HOPE
STREET

HOPE STREET

AMANDA ANDRUZZI

Edited by:
JAMES RATZLAFF

Archway Publishing books may be ordered through booksellers or by contacting:

Archway Publishing
1663 Liberty Drive
Bloomington, IN 47403
www.archwaypublishing.com
1-(888)-242-5904

Because of the dynamic nature of the Internet, any web addresses or links contained in this book may have changed since publication and may no longer be valid. The views expressed in this work are solely those of the author and do not necessarily reflect the views of the publisher, and the publisher hereby disclaims any responsibility for them.

Any people depicted in stock imagery provided by Thinkstock are models, and such images are being used for illustrative purposes only.

Certain stock imagery © Thinkstock.

ISBN: 978-1-4808-0084-7 (sc)
ISBN: 978-1-4808-0086-1 (hc)
ISBN: 978-1-4808-0085-4 (e)

Library of Congress Control Number: 2013908935

Printed in the United States of America

Archway Publishing rev. date: 5/21/2013

I dedicate this book to my daughter,

Sage

INTRODUCTION: OUR STORY

As a child, I used to wake in the night to the sounds of my mother screaming at my father. She was violent in her words, and I was scared. I remember seeing police officers in our living room on a number of occasions. One officer with a very kind face looked at me with deep brown eyes and the saddest expression I had ever seen, as if he were trying to tell me he was sorry but there was nothing he could do. I always preferred kindness from a stranger over that from my own parents; theirs made me uncomfortable.

I learned how to spend time at other houses at a very young age. I spent most of my summer vacations with my extended family and the families of friends. I must have seemed like a permanent fixture in their homes and at their tables. Only with them did I feel like a kid with no cares or worries. For a young girl, I worried a lot, and I always started to worry when it was time to go home.

I knew my parents loved me, but I don't think they knew how to be parents. I lived day to day, hour to hour, never knowing when there would be violence: shouting in the middle of the night or a plate shattered on the kitchen floor. If there was peace for a little while, I didn't trust it. I grew up scared, lonely, and sad, and had very low self-esteem.

But instead of becoming angry and defiant, I did the opposite. I did well in school, got my first job at the age of twelve, and continued to work until the day I left for college. I never gave my parents any problems. Although I dated and fooled around, I wasn't having sex, and I wasn't involved with drugs in any way. I was scared of drugs. I would drink occasionally—and maybe even a little too much my first year of college—but it was always for fun, and it never interrupted my life.

I guess I don't carry the addiction gene, and I was frightened by anyone who did. I distanced myself from a lot of my friends when I saw them red-eyed and spacey, or talking too fast. I was insecure, but not enough to cloud myself in a haze of white powder and smoke.

When I first met Jim, I was nineteen years old, and he was twenty-three. He had been a good friend of my cousin Jason since childhood, but I had somehow never met him; or maybe I just didn't remember him—we were four years apart, after all, and when you are young, that seems like a lifetime. My grandmother and aunt, whom I adored, liked Jim a lot, and it was my grandmother who set us up.

I was home from college for the summer, and just came home from working as a nanny when my phone rang. My grandmother said she had someone who wanted to speak to me, and she put Jim on the phone. I had seen Jim at her house earlier that week but we barely spoke. I was on the spot, but was instantly relieved when I heard how nervous he sounded on the other end of the line. He asked me if I wanted to go out with him that night, and I reluctantly agreed.

We planned a double date for a movie with my best friend Jackie and her boyfriend, Ray. I was waiting with them when a motorcycle pulled up and the rider stepped off. When he walked toward us and pulled his helmet off, I saw Jim's warm, dimpled smile and his clear green eyes that seemed to change color before me, and my reluctance began to slip away. I can still picture him from those days: tanned, lean, and muscular, with a slight cleft in his chin. It was strange that I had never noticed him before.

We went to a bar after the movie, and I asked Jim why he had asked me out.

"Well," he said, "I think you're beautiful." He looked me straight in the eye. "I've wanted to ask you for a while, but I didn't want to stir things up with your family. Your grandmother's persistent, though." He smiled. "I wasn't sure you'd say yes, but I'm glad you did."

I was glad, too, although it took a couple weeks for me to realize that he was growing on me. I was young and pretty, educated and intelligent, but insecure. I had never had a problem dating or attracting men, but I always lost interest after a few weeks. I had never forged a strong connection with any man, probably because I never felt good enough about myself to let anybody in very deep. But with Jim, I felt that changing.

We soon became inseparable. We laughed and went on vacations together and wanted to be around each other all the time. He was supportive, loving, caring, and hysterically funny; he was smart and handsome. He knew what he wanted, which was very attractive to me. He always seemed to have money, and he paid for everything. He decided to go back to college, and he quit smoking. At twenty-three, he had already been to rehab for cocaine addiction and had been clean for four years. He said he never had a problem with alcohol. He was very open and honest about everything, which I, at the time, believed was actually a good thing.

We were genuinely in love, but toward the end of our first three years, I could see a different person developing in Jim. He seemed to be telling lies, even about little things that didn't matter. He was unmotivated, depressed, anxiety-ridden, and lazy. I had a prescription for Xanax a doctor had given me from a time in high school when I had suffered from panic attacks. It was still full—I don't like pills—and when Jim had anxiety, I would offer him one because I didn't know how else to help him. He took them gratefully—at my request, of course.

He told me he was enrolled at my college in a special program that would allow him to attend nights and graduate. And it just so happened that every time he had class, I did, too. I never saw his car in the parking lot. There were times I saw him driving away from the school when he should have been driving toward it.

His books and his work seldom materialized—they always seemed to be "in the car," and I eventually had to ask him about it. I came home one day, and he showed me a paper he had written for one of his classes. It was actually pretty good, and I couldn't imagine that anyone would write a ten-page paper for a class that didn't exist. I put my suspicions away for the time being.

Yet it wasn't long before I passed his house, and his car was there when it should have been at school. I called to ask him about it, but had to leave my question on his answering machine. I begged him to tell me if he was really enrolled in college or if this was all a lie. He denied my claims vehemently. He called me twenty minutes later from a pay phone at the college and had a passerby get on the phone and verify he was at school. Then why was his car at his house? Was I seeing things? I wanted to believe him.

There were other signs. He began smoking again and trying, unsuccessfully, to hide it from me. He drank; he was by no means a drunk, but he did drink, and in retrospect, this should have worried me. He had lethargic friends who seemed to need nothing more out of life than a couch and a television set. But I was too busy with my own life to spend all my time monitoring his: I worked full-time and took as many classes as I could handle in order to graduate.

It was when I was finishing college, about to graduate with highest honors, that something terrible happened.

I hadn't seen Jim for a few days, which was strange. He called one night from "a friend's" house, and I couldn't get a word in edgewise as he talked to me. Though he spoke of grandiose schemes and bragged about people who wanted to work with him and the money he was going to make, his voice was stone-cold. He didn't sound like the person I knew, and I hung up worried. He called again at six o'clock the next morning, and my mother had to tell him that I was still sleeping. When I awoke, she said he had sounded strange. In what seemed like an effort to make things better, a few months earlier, we bought a Boxer puppy together. Sadie was with me that morning at my mother's house.

I was angry, and when I went to his apartment to drop off our dog before work, I almost didn't even go in. I almost just let the dog in and walked away, but something told me to look inside. I poked my head in and saw him: he was sitting on the couch, his face gray. I called his name and got no response. I screamed it. An infomercial prattled away on the television set in front of him.

He just sat there, upright but frozen, in a flannel shirt, ripped jeans, boots, and a baseball cap. He looked like a corpse, but his lungs were gasping for air. He was unconscious. I shook him. I slapped him across the face to wake him up: "Jim! Jim, can you hear me? It's me, Amanda!"

Nothing.

I pulled up his eyelids, and his eyes were rolled far back in his head. I could hardly believe this wasn't a nightmare, that it was really happening. My mind froze and I didn't know what to do, but my body took over. I shook him again and I tried giving him mouth-to-mouth resuscitation, smearing brown lipstick on his face as I did so.

Nothing worked. He was apparently in a coma, barely breathing and cold. He was asphyxiating.

I called 9-1-1, and I also called my cousin Angie and her husband, Amjed, who was a doctor; they lived around the corner and came over in three minutes. He tried mouth-to-mouth as well and got no response. We felt helpless as we waited for the ambulance to arrive.

When it did and the EMTs asked me what he was on, I froze. I had no answer. I blurted out, "Cocaine." It was all he had ever really talked about doing. The EMT said it looked like a heroin overdose, and I said that was impossible, that he wasn't into heroin. But what did I know?

They immediately pulled out a large syringe and plunged the needle into his chest. The shot of adrenaline woke him instantly. He bolted upright like a body in a morgue rising from the dead, looked around for nearly a minute, and said, "What the fuck is going on?"

"Sir," said one of the EMTs, "you had a drug overdose, and we are here to help you. What did you take?"

"I don't know what the fuck you're talking about."

"Sir, your girlfriend called us because you were not responding."

"I'm fine," he said. He tried to stand up but lost his balance.

They strapped him to a gurney and put him in the ambulance; they told me that if I had arrived fifteen minutes later—just fifteen minutes—he would have been dead. I rode with him to the hospital. I didn't want to lose him; all the love that had faded out of me in the last few months came rushing back. I wanted to be with him and take care of him more than anything else. I don't know why, but I felt somehow responsible for him: he was broken, and I needed to help fix him.

"Go the fuck home," he said to me at the hospital an hour later. They wanted to keep him a while longer for observation. "I don't need you here. *I* don't need to be here."

"Jim," I said, "you overdosed." He had been nasty and abusive the whole time we had been there, and I was shocked. I didn't know where his anger was coming from.

"What?" he said. "I didn't do shit. I'm fine. I need a cigarette." He looked around the emergency room. "When can I get out of here?"

"They need to run some more tests. You were in a coma, Jim. You almost died."

He seemed to soften then. "Yeah, okay. Whatever. I need a cigarette."

I finally left. I couldn't believe he was attacking me. When I went back to his apartment while he was in the hospital, I found a hollowed-out pen in the pocket of his pants; there was white powder on it. I was horrified and felt defeated. He was my first love—my first everything—and I knew nothing about addiction. I loved him, and I thought that was enough.

When he came home from the hospital, he slept for almost two days. I stayed at the apartment with him, sleeping on the love seat by his side.

When he finally came to, he admitted that he was really depressed and unmotivated. I decided to wait it out with him and see what happened. We weren't together, but we were still spending a lot of time with each other and I was trying to help him as much as I could.

He was still insisting that he was going to graduate college in a "special program." I decided to call the school and find out if the program even existed. It didn't, and neither did his professor, Professor Rubenstien. Rubenstien was also the name Jim used for the therapist he was supposedly seeing. Nothing was adding up. Then I realized something, Doctor Rubenstien was the name of a veterinarian we had seen a while back. Why was I only putting the pieces together now? I called him from work, so disgusted I didn't want to even look at him. This whole situation was insane, literally insane.

For the next two months, I kept in contact with him; we would meet and sleep together on occasion, but it just felt too sad. Eventually, after he started to get better, I broke up with him and moved on.

I moved into an apartment with roommates in Manhattan. I got a job at a public relations firm and never felt better. I met someone and dated him for seven months. It was pretty serious and we really liked each other, but there was always something missing.

Jim remained a family friend, and I would still see him from time to time—we shared "custody" of our dog.

My aunt was dying of stomach cancer, and I had an awful time watching her suffer. She was also my godmother, and we had always been close: along with my grandmother, she practically raised me. She was fun and calm and spontaneous, and I loved and adored her. I came home every weekend to be with her and didn't want to let her go. I spent as much time as I could with her that year. We laughed a lot and talked a lot, and I cried in private a lot, not wanting her to see that I knew she was dying.

I watched her go from a vibrant woman to a skeleton over a period of six months, during which she had two surgeries where they cut her open from neck to pelvis. I remember thinking how strong she was. No matter how sick she was, she was still concerned about me.

One day I helped her get dressed. She had never been overweight, but she had always been a full-bodied woman. Now, standing next to me before the mirror in her bedroom, she was literally skin and bones. I tried to swallow the lump in my throat, but I couldn't and tears fell down my face. I tried to hold them back, but she saw me. I think she knew then that I knew how this was going to end.

During her last few months, I helped to nurse, clean, and feed her, and I sat by her side as much as I could until the very end. One day I was out of her room for less than a minute, and when her daughter walked back in, she was already gone. She chose the moment when no one was with her to pass on. A part of me died that day, and when I gave her eulogy, there was not a dry eye in the entire church. I spoke from the heart and didn't have to embellish one word.

While this was going on, Jim was there for me in ways I didn't think were possible. He was getting his life back together, looking, feeling, and acting like the man I had first fallen in love with. We slowly started talking and were soon back together. Something about the way he held me, the way he wrapped his arms around me, made me feel so safe.

I was afraid of drugs and what he had done, but I felt as though what had happened nine months earlier had not really happened, that the man with me now was a different person. I hadn't thought anyone could come back from that place; I didn't think the person I was seeing now could ever come back, but here he was: *my* Jim.

He was strident about being honest and open and said he would do nothing that could compromise his sobriety. He resolved not to drink for one year. He was serious about restoring his life, our life. I respected his honesty, his mission, his sense of purpose. He seemed positive that he had the answers, that he wasn't like other drug addicts because he knew he needed help and freely admitted it.

The next couple years were better. He was working and doing well, and I was working, too. I really loved him, and I know he loved me. We moved in together. Things weren't perfect, but I never saw signs of drugs. He told me little lies about smoking cigarettes here and there, but that didn't worry me. The one sign that I look back on now that should have told me he could relapse was that he never did give up drinking. He was never out of control, though, so I figured it was okay. He would sometimes have a drink or two when we went out, but that was it. I never saw him drunk in those days.

Two years into our renewed relationship, Jim asked me to—in front of my whole family in Manhattan on Christmas Eve—to marry him. I said yes, despite our difficulties, because I couldn't imagine spending my life with anyone else. I was happy, and I put his addiction out of my mind. We bought a house, moved in together, renovated it, and I became pregnant. I still felt a distance between us, like we still weren't entirely on the same page, but I chose to focus not on the past but on what we had here and now, and what we had was a little miracle.

Our daughter Sage's arrival was a monumentally life-changing experience for me. The moment she was born, I wanted nothing but to be absolutely the best mother I could be for her. I instantly fell in love with her, with my new family. This was something that was my own, something I helped create.

Jim, though, was a different story. He was generally happy to be a father, but he was far from engaged. I had seen other children run into the arms of their dads when they got home from work, but that didn't happen here. There was an aloofness about him, always a distance. I attributed this to his relationship with his own father, who used drugs, cheated on his mother, and abandoned him for ten years. When his father returned an alcoholic, still using drugs and penniless, he borrowed money from Jim and never paid it back. When he died, he left Jim with the funeral bill.

Sage was eighteen months old when Jim's father died. Soon after, on two occasions, I found pills on him, which he said belonged to someone else, pointing out that he hadn't taken them, had he? I was naïve, and the truth was, he never did look high. Then again, what did I know? I had never used a drug in my life. The doctors had to force Tylenol with codeine on me when I had a very painful C-section; I barely even took that.

I was overwhelmed with a baby that Jim didn't really help me out with. I thought that his almost dying and having a child would have been all he needed to never take drugs again. We had a series of heart-to-heart talks, where he told me he never wanted to be like his father. It was three weeks before his next relapse.

Jim and some friends went overnight to Atlantic City on business. This was a first. I was home with our daughter. He didn't call me, and he didn't answer my calls, which wasn't like him at all. When I finally did get him on the phone, he spoke to me as if I were a business associate, very matter-of-factly.

The next day I took our daughter to my parents' house and waited at home for him with a drug test, shaking. He was obviously high, but he claimed he was clean even as he took the test in front of me. It came up positive for Xanax, cocaine, and marijuana. He swore on our daughter's life that he had not taken anything and that I was crazy. But he was so disoriented that when he left the house, he actually tried to get into our neighbor's car. I told him never to come home such a wreck. I remember the next words he said to me as if he said them to me yesterday:

"Get away from me. *I don't love you.*"

I just turned and walked away. I stayed with my parents for a week. This was a side of my husband I had never seen before. When he was on drugs, it was like there was ice water running through his veins.

After a week, he was feeling better and was very apologetic and willing to work on our marriage and get help.

I found a $5,000 charge on his credit card for lingerie; he swore he was just buying it for a business associate who was cheating on his wife. (Like that was all right?) He said he loved me more than anything in the whole world and didn't want to be without me, that there was no way he ever would or could cheat on me. And besides, he knew I looked at our credit card statements, so he would never be stupid enough to leave such an obvious trail. These were all words I wanted to hear. I fell for it hook, line, and sinker.

A couple months later, we went away for a night with our daughter, and he was acting strange, saying his back hurt and that he was tired. He slept almost the entire trip. I should have known something was up, but I couldn't believe he would lie to me that much or get high in front of his daughter. I didn't know what to make of it, so I chose not to make anything of it at all.

What I didn't see was that he was a very high-functioning addict. He rarely went out and generally spent a lot of time with us, but he put space between us by lying and never sharing his day-to-day feelings. He was beginning to lead a double life.

One day, a couple of months after his relapse in Atlantic City, I watched as he shook like a leaf, his legs going into spasms. I had to sit him in a bathtub of hot water because he couldn't stop shaking. He was detoxing from pills, and even as I watched him do it, he denied it to the point of no return. I wanted to believe him. I didn't want to see. I didn't have the energy to fight anymore.

Things got much better before they got much worse. We moved from our house into an apartment in Manhattan so I could be closer to my school. For that year, our relationship was the best it had ever been. I stopped complaining to my friends about our marriage, and I was able to focus on myself and raising our daughter. We spent a lot of time together and were very happy.

We lived in a huge two-bedroom apartment on the ground floor of a brownstone. It had thirteen-foot ceilings and a 700-square-foot deck with Japanese shrubs and lights, just off our bedroom. It had two bathrooms, a washer and dryer, and a kitchen that overlooked the whole open space of our living and dining rooms.

We were living an amazing life, and paying for it. Our bills, before any spending money—and we spent a *lot*—were over $14,000 a month, and I paid them without batting an eyelash. I did ask how he was making so much money, and he answered in such a way that I really believed he was a genius, an amazing businessman for whom money would never be an issue. By the time I was done asking him to show me our bank statements and what he was doing, he would turn things around so much that I would forget what my original question was. After weeks of promises, I just got tired of asking.

He did acknowledge, though, that our outrageous spending habits probably weren't sustainable just yet, so after a year, we moved back into our house on Staten Island. Things were okay for a few months, but it still bothered me that he drank occasionally, he never went to NA meetings, and he stopped seeing his therapist. After Jim's overdose, I started reading about addiction. I had gone to the bookstore and looked around the addiction and co-addiction section. I learned that an addict should always be aware of and working on his recovery, but he had me convinced again that his relapse was just a fluke.

Over the next year, his business life was obviously a struggle for him because he always seemed stressed about work, and it remained a mystery to me, too, even though I begged him to open up to me. He said it was just the stress of closing a huge deal that would change our lives. He said he wanted to "show" me rather than tell me, and he did: less than a year after we moved back, we sold our little house and moved into a 7,000-square-foot home in the best neighborhood on Staten Island. It was on the top of a hill, and the back was all windows overlooking the eastern side of the island, the Bridge, and the water. The house had every amenity possible: two kitchens, four bedrooms, five bathrooms, a swimming pool, a pool table, and a wine cellar. My dream bathroom came complete with cathedral ceilings in a round room with a two-person Jacuzzi and a separate shower that was also a steam room. I was floored. I fell in love with the place instantly. (Believe it or not, this house was a compromise: it was only two million dollars; Jim had originally wanted me to look at houses in the four-million-dollar range.) We used the $50,000 equity from our original house as a down payment and moved in immediately.

I wish I could say that living in this paradise made things better between us, but it didn't. In fact, they got worse. We started to try and have another baby so Jim needed to stop his hormone therapy for low testosterone. Although he was young, he was not producing enough of the right hormones. Because Jim had lapsed in taking his libido medication for the past year or so, things began once again to spiral out of control. He was lethargic, lazy, sexually unavailable, and distant all over again. I was scared and tried to give him all the resources he needed to get help, but when he would pretend to use them or lie, I would just become angry, and he would turn my anger around to make me look bad or crazy.

Four months after moving into this beautiful house with this family that I would do anything to protect, I noticed signs that Jim was using something. Until this point, I had only seen horrible, short relapses; I had never known him to use habitually for long periods of time—or so I thought. His eyes started to droop at the dinner table, and he began to distance himself from Sage and me to the point where he started sleeping on the couch in the basement to be alone. He got into a number of car accidents, one of which was right in front of our house, where he bashed our truck into a stone wall. He claimed that a stray dog had run in front of the car. (There were no stray dogs in our neighborhood.) He had an illegal and unregistered gun that he took to bed with him in the basement. I did not know if he was becoming paranoid or if something else was going on.

He told me he was developing a building on Hope Street in Manhattan and that he was running into one problem after another, but that everything would be okay and that when all was said and done, we would be set for life. For the next six months, we flip-flopped between fighting and trying to make up and start over. All the while he was on prescription drugs, but I couldn't prove it. I was living in a nightmare. He was lying and making me feel depressed, irritable, insecure, and scared. I felt like I was losing my mind.

In February 2009, I had booked a family trip to Disney World. Things were escalating, and he was acting stranger all the time. One day he would be wonderful, the husband I always knew he could be; the next he would be distant; and the next he would dismiss me if there was any confrontation. One day we would be a loving husband and wife, and the next he would be telling me he was leaving me because he couldn't take me anymore.

Four days before the Florida trip, he told me he couldn't go because he had an important inspection for his building that he couldn't reschedule. I had told him earlier that before we left, I wanted to see that he had no drugs with him; if he was clean for a whole week, I could believe he was not using. I was sure now he didn't want to come because it would mean he couldn't bring drugs with him. I tried to talk with him and even resorted to writing my feelings in e-mails to him, but he wouldn't budge. I told him he should live well for Sage, but nothing seemed to resonate. When I said I would cancel the trip, he told me I should go alone with her or take my father. I took my dad, but I was sad that Sage wasn't able to experience Disney World with her own father.

I called him the first night we were there, and he sounded groggy and slurred his words. He denied being high, as usual, and I didn't see the point of letting him upset me any further. By the end of the trip, I had talked to him quite a few times, and he never sounded much better.

The day we were coming home, my mother called and said there were some problems between Jim and my cousin Jason, who had introduced us. They had done some business together, and Jason wanted money that he claimed Jim owed him. While I was gone, Jason had told the family that Jim was using drugs and acting strange.

I called another cousin who had spoken to Jim; she said he was belligerent and angry and wouldn't let her get a word in edgewise. I knew this behavior; it was all too familiar. I tried to get Jim on the phone from Orlando. It was a Saturday at noon, and I knew he never slept past six in the morning. He didn't answer the house phone or his cell phone.

During the time we had been trying to get pregnant we decided it was time to start using a fertility specialist. In January, the doctor recommended that I try artificial insemination with Jim's sperm. The first time we tried, he had to ejaculate into a cup. That morning I dropped Sage off at school while he tried to give his sample. When I came back to take the sample to the doctor, I found him frustrated and angry because he was unable to ejaculate. I suspected that drugs were the problem, and I got angry myself. I yelled at him. He blew up right back and threw the sample cup at me, calling me horrible names I don't even want to recall.

I calmed down and realized I still had the appointment to keep, so I talked to him … and even tried to help him … but he just couldn't do it. Even though I knew it wasn't my fault, I felt like a failure—again.

His lying and abuse were affecting every aspect of our life, destroying all the good things I thought we had. He blamed his failure and behavior on low testosterone levels and started taking his prescribed hormones again. I wanted to believe that this was the real problem and that by starting the treatment again, we would get our family back.

Shortly before I left for Disney World, we tried another artificial insemination, which was unsuccessful. It never occurred to me that he would try to have a baby with me while he was on drugs. Even he wouldn't jeopardize the health of his unborn child that way—would he? I thought that maybe I really had been crazy, because no one could be that selfish. Lying, hurting, and deceiving me was one thing, but compromising the safety of an innocent life was below even him.

He started going to NA meetings again like when he went to rehabilitation at the age of nineteen, and resumed seeing a therapist in the city. I appreciated his efforts, and we decided to try and save our family. Nevertheless, things got a lot worse. I don't know if I was a typical enabler, because I never made excuses for him or his drug abuse to our friends or family. But he was so manipulative that he always had me believing he was doing the right thing—or at least trying very hard.

For the next three months, we worked at being a family again, but something was always off. His eyes would sag, he slurred his words, and his pupils were tiny, but I still couldn't prove anything and he wouldn't budge. He even had his doctor write me a letter stating that he was free of all substances in his drug test with regard to his "treatment". I immediately questioned this and knew that his treatment probably involved other drugs, but I still had no evidence.

I opened a letter to Jim, from our health insurance company, making him aware that they were in the process of requesting authorization for an oxycodone prescription from his doctor in the city. My heart sank into my stomach. Jim said it was a request *to test* for oxycodone, not to prescribe it. When I called the insurance company, they said the prescription had not been filled. But my gut just kept churning, no matter how hard I tried to believe him. I searched his car and only found cigarette boxes, which I confronted him with. I forgave him for lying to me about smoking and told him it was okay to be honest with me, to please just tell me the truth. Even after I thought the cigarettes were why he was lying and acting strange, I still couldn't get the sick feeling out of my stomach.

On a hunch, I called our insurance company again and played dumb. I told them I needed to pick up my husband's medications but didn't know at which pharmacy. They gave me the number to the pharmacy, and I played dumb again. I reiterated the same story and they said, "Not to worry, Mrs. Andruzzi. Your husband already picked up his prescriptions for oxycodone and Xanax."

Chapter 1: The Beginning of the End—April 2009

How do I live with someone who treats me like I'm not part of his life? How does he expect me not to get angry, to have any trust in him whatsoever? He's been deceiving me openly for months, maybe even years, and it would be insane to not react and feel anger.

Today I found Xanax right out in the open on his shelf. I couldn't have missed it if I tried. There it was, a big 2-mg stick thrown in with his spare change. We spoke when he got home, and he reluctantly agreed to get help. We're sleeping separately now.

April 22, 2009

It's been eight weeks and counting since Jim and I have slept together, and seven weeks living in misery with Jim's anger, mood swings, and brief moments of clarity. I know he's not a bad person. I wouldn't have married a bad person. His heart can't be that depraved, but I can't help but be angry at him for being the world's shittiest dad. Any father who uses drugs in front of his child is hardly a father at all.

I was listening to the radio on my way back from driving Sage to school this morning, and there was a program on about relationships. A therapist was talking about three things that you need for a good relationship: communication (we don't have that), respect (don't have that either), and trust (we definitely don't have that). We had the love, we definitely did, but we no longer have the sex or passion that at least makes the rest palatable.

We have distance, loneliness, and a growing disdain for one another.

We saw a therapist on Monday for the first time. He was great and has personal and professional experience with drug addiction. He called Jim out every time he lied or acted as an addict in our session. Jim would say something that I knew was bullshit, and the therapist would say, "Is that Jim talking, or is that Drug Addict Jim talking?" It made me feel great—not to see someone hurting him, but to see someone else seeing what I see. I could finally breathe. I wasn't alone, and I wasn't overreacting. I'm not crazy.

Before the second session, Jim announced that he wanted a divorce. We had always said that if either one of us, at any point, didn't want to go on anymore, we should say so right away. I didn't think it would be this soon, but I guess after I accused him again of using in front of our daughter, he had had enough; to be honest, I had, too.

The following are e-mails between Jim and me after our second counseling session.

From: Amanda
Date: Tuesday, April 21, 2009 1:10 PM
To: Jim
Subject: Hi!

I know I said it last night, but I want to say it again since it's hard for us to really talk to each other without getting bitter and angry. I just want you to know how sorry I am for all of this. I never wanted for things to be this way. Lately all I have been seeing is the bad side of you, and I'm sure you feel the same way about me; now, I regret to say, I have shut out the good because the bad is so overwhelming.

I know you have a good heart. I know you mean well and that you are in no way a bad person, just someone with a lot of problems and addictions I can't help with. The hardest part is sitting by and watching the man I love destroy himself, going deeper and deeper into a dark place and taking for granted the life we have. Or had. I get angry, like I'm waving a sign in front of you to tell you to snap out of it, and you're ignoring me. But I realize it's not that simple.

You made a very hard decision a few days ago, and I admire you for it—I know it must not have been easy. It's something I haven't had the courage to say, but I know this situation isn't healthy for either of us. I miss so greatly who you used to be. I've been trying so hard to make you better that I lost sight of the bigger picture. I can't make you better, and I was drowning myself in the process.

I'll get my strength back, slowly but surely, and our daughter will always be Number One on my list of priorities. I'll spend my whole life making sure she is safe and secure and feels loved, no matter what happens with you. Even if it's just for a little while, a month or whatever, maybe we should separate: I can't live with such anger and hatred. Neither of us deserves that, and Sage especially doesn't.

I know you think I talk a lot and repeat myself, so I'm sorry if this e-mail annoys you or is redundant. I just don't know how to do this. I don't know how to cut all ties and not care about you anymore; so maybe this note is more for me than you. I don't know. I know these are just words, but they are true.

Amanda

Jim wrote back to me shortly after. He said he knew he released a lot of anger on me last night and that he was sorry, that he felt the same way, but he deals with his frustrations in his life very differently. He said the main thing was we both deal with these problems completely the wrong way and both of us become destructive to ourselves as well as to each other. He said the decision he made was the hardest and most unselfish thing he had done in all his life because he loved our daughter and me more than anything in this world, and he saw no other way to protect us from what was turning uglier by the minute. He swore he was doing all he could to deal with his addictions and slumps of depression and that it had been impossible before, without the help he was finally getting for himself.

He went on to say he never wanted to lose me, but as he tried to help himself get better and become a better person, he was watching me fall apart. He said I was not getting the help I needed to overcome my issues because I had been completely focused on him; this is what made him realize that with him in my life, I might never help myself. He claimed the only way to give me a chance to get better for me and for Sage's sake was to leave. He said he hated having to leave me, and he would give up everything if he thought I could move forward and better my life with him in it, but he didn't see that I could do that with him like he was able to do it with me. He said he loved me and wanted no one else but me, but it seemed as long as he was around, I wasn't myself. He was sorry things had gotten to this point, and it was something that would haunt him forever. He signed it, *Love, Jim,* and that was it.

From: Amanda
Date: Tuesday, April 21, 2009 5:45 PM
To: Jim
Subject: Re: Hi!

Your addiction and ability to be deceitful bring out the worst in me. I am not myself. The only time I feel okay is when I don't have to see you and what you're going through. We don't know how to fight, make up, and move forward, rely deeply on each other, or be truly vulnerable or close. Some couples get together in times of crisis, but we tear each other apart. I just couldn't bear to give up on our family, but I understand. I get it, I do. But that doesn't make it any easier to swallow.

Monday, May 11, 2009

Yesterday was Mother's Day. Jim and I have decided to try to work things out for the sake of our family and for Sage. I can barely rationalize why I continue to try with him anymore except that we are husband and wife, and we promised to love each other for better or worse.

We hosted breakfast at our house for our mothers. Jim bought me the GPS unit I wanted, and he was pleasant and helpful all day. After dinner he said he wanted to go hiking with us girls, which made me happy. But as we were getting changed, he began complaining, saying he was tired and that his back hurt. When I asked if he still wanted to come, he said no, that he'd like to stay home and rest. I wish I could say I was surprised.

I'm pretty sure he got high while we were out. When we spoke that night, his eyes were closing in mid-sentence. That's not normal, is it?

I went to sleep exhausted. In the middle of the night, I woke from a horrible nightmare. I was relieved to be out of the dream until I realized where I was.

My real life is worse than my nightmares.

Chapter 2: Addicted to Him—July 2009

From: Amanda
Date: Fri, 10 Jul 2009 5:17 PM
To: Jim
Subject: [no subject]

Jim,

We have to figure out a way to make this work for Sage. I didn't mean to lash out at you last night, but I don't know what else to do anymore. You have completely broken my heart. I feel dead inside. I know deep down that you are never going to change for me or for yourself, but maybe you will for her.

I now see so much of your father in you. You're not a bad person, and neither was he; he just lived by his addictions. But even if you take the drugs away, the behavior is still there. Life itself is never good enough—you don't know what it is to feel like yourself anymore. I don't even know if you know who you are—you're too busy distracting yourself and everyone else from seeing the dark parts inside you. You've kept me at a distance our whole relationship, always hiding some major part of your life from me.

The part that reminds me so much of your father is that you're plagued by your addictions: food, drugs, cigarettes—whatever it is, you can't stop that addictive behavior, and that's why it's crucial to be honest. Like you said about the cigarettes, at first you just have one here or there, and then before you know it, you're smoking full-on. Lies work that way, too. How many times did you look at your father and say, "If he could just stop acting like that or stop the drugs and drinking, he could have a real life?" Well, that's how I feel about you.

You're 35 years old and still battling addiction, still hiding from your wife, still bingeing on cookies and nicotine. What kind of example is this for our daughter? If she were doing the things you're doing at 35, you would be devastated—at least I hope you would. If she were married to an addict who lied to her and hurt her, you would probably kill him. You would never want her to be like you, never.

I can only be the best mother I can be, but I can't be the only one to set a good example. She's the product of both her parents, and if one of them lives by his addictive behaviors, that is going to mold who she becomes!

Remember going through your father's things after he died and finding the needle kit for heroin, when you thought he was clean? Well, maybe it won't be in a one-room apartment—maybe it will be in a beautiful condo or a mansion, it doesn't matter—but I'm afraid for you. Your behavior will kill you if you don't stop.

I looked up the criteria for "pathological liar" to try and understand what might be going on, and this is what I found.

1) They "construct" a reality around themselves. They don't value the truth, especially if they don't see their lies as hurting anyone.

2) They tend toward hypochondria. This can come in especially useful when caught in a lie: they can claim that they've been sick, or that there's some mysterious "illness" that has them all stressed-out.

3) They contradict what they say. This becomes very clear over time. They usually aren't smart enough to keep track of so many lies. (Who would be?)

You exhibit all of these behaviors. I also looked up the behavior of a typical co-dependent or co-addict, and I fit the criteria for all of that. This is a vicious cycle.

Jim, I look into our little girl's eyes and it changes my whole world, makes me strive to be the best person I can be, and of course, I want her father to be his best whether I'm with him or not. Get better for her. Just look into her eyes and watch her smile, and let that give you strength, because right now I don't think you feel good enough about yourself to do it for you.

You want to spend a day with her alone, but what are you going to do—run away every hour for a cigarette because you don't want her to know you smoke? What kind of life is that? You expect the truth out of her, you get angry if she lies, yet you don't expect it from yourself. What are you showing her?

I thought if I loved you enough or if you could see how much you're hurting me, it would make you stop, but now I can see I was wrong. You saw a woman last night who had nothing left to lose, broken heart-and-soul. I never thought I could feel so empty. You've taken my love for you and this family and made it ugly, and I let you. But I won't repeat the pattern you've created. Unlike your mother, I'll never let Sage see the sadness in me—never—but I won't cover up for you. Take what I'm saying not as a heartless criticism or cruel way of making you feel bad about yourself. Take what I am saying as if your life depended on it, because it does.

Amanda

He didn't e-mail me back, but he did
acknowledge that we needed to talk.

Sunday, July 19, 2009

I'm not paranoid. At least I have that. What a couple of days.

Yesterday Jim finally agreed to let me go with him to see the drug counselor he's been seeing since March. When we met outside the counselor's office in Manhattan, he said he couldn't come in, that something had come up. I didn't believe him and convinced him to go in, which is where things continued to go wrong.

He was supposed to be going twice a week for the last four months, but the counselor, Mark, hardly seemed to know him: "I've barely seen you," he said. Jim tried to change the subject, but the counselor remained professional and wouldn't budge.

After about ten minutes Jim left in a rage, yelling, "You're lying! You're going to hear from my lawyer!" It was hard to see, but I can't say I was surprised. What did surprise me was when the counselor told me that Jim was plainly lying and that he felt Jim was using these visits as an excuse to tell me what I wanted to hear. He actually told me I should get out of this relationship, that Jim was a very sick individual. I don't know why, but I still didn't want to give up.

(I do know why, of course: it was for our family, for Sage.)

That night I got Jim to agree to go with me to a family party, where I staged an impromptu intervention. Even this he managed to turn around on me. It was my mom, my dad, and my cousin Angie, and they basically sat him down and said, "What's up?"

Jim sat right down with them, looked them each in the eye, and told them I was making it all up. He said he would happily take a urine test for them, which he did, with the full knowledge that he was on drugs and would be found out. I couldn't believe it.

But when he walked out, my own family actually looked at me like *I* was the crazy one, and asked me if I was really sure I was seeing what I thought I was seeing. They asked if maybe I was imagining it. I couldn't breathe. I felt like the ground had been torn out from under me.

When I got home that night, he was already passed out.

The next morning, Saturday, Jim said he had to go out for work and asked Sage to go with him on a two-hour drive he had to take. Jim never worked Saturdays. I told him Sage going with him might be a good idea, knowing full well he had no intention on taking her. He asked if I would check and see if his wallet was in our bedroom. I initially went up the stairs but stopped myself halfway up. When I looked back, I could see his wallet outline in his jeans as he walked the other way. I ran back down the stairs to find him sneaking pills out of our boiler room. I asked him to show me what was in his hands, and he hid them behind his back—actually hid them behind his back like a child!

"What are you holding?" I asked him.

"Nothing!" he said.

"Then why won't you show me?"

"It's none of your goddamn business!" This, in front of our daughter.

I told Sage to stay where she was and followed him up the stairs. I was shaking and begged him to admit it—I just needed him to look me in the face and tell me I was not crazy. He grabbed me by my arms and threw me across the bedroom. I began to cry and told him to stop, because our daughter was home. Finally he said, "I need these. I can't just stop; I'm weaning off of them. They're prescriptions from my doctor."

I followed him downstairs to his car, all the while thinking: *What am I doing? I'm acting just as unstable as he is!* I felt like he was tearing my heart right out of my chest. The engine was running, and I opened the door to talk to him. He drove away while I was still half in the car. I was thrown onto the cement garage floor and scraped both my hands. He raced up the driveway and didn't even look back to see if I was okay. Bloodied and raw, I lifted the palms of my hands from the course pavement. Trembling, I choked back my tears, and stood up.

I ran inside and tried to calm Sage, who was distraught. Up until then, I had always felt after we fought that we would get over it, that it would be okay again soon—but not this time. This was my defining moment. I knew right then that there was no going back. I had to leave this man, or he would destroy my daughter and me over his little white pills. Twelve years, one overdose, one child, and three "confirmed" relapses later, I had finally had it.

I told my friend Jackie recently that I was afraid to do the laundry. My heart feels like it's in my stomach because I have to go through his pockets and I'm afraid of what I might find. Same goes for cleaning the house. This is no way to live, and now that I can finally see that it's affecting our daughter, I'm left with no choice.

I've lost eight pounds in three days, and I look skinny and sick. I can barely get through a sentence without crying. I am mourning him. But I know I will get strong—having Sage gives me no choice. I'll never make up for the emotional abandonment of her father, but I'll do the best I can.

I'll do the best I can and just hope it is enough.

Wednesday, July 22, 2009

The last few days, Jim has been lazing around the house in a fog. He's agreed to go into detox. Since we're getting a divorce, he doesn't want me to use it against him if he doesn't. I was silently relieved. I tried to keep Sage away from him yesterday. He was so out of it that when he went to the trunk of his car to get his drugs, he dropped the oxycodone. He actually asked me to help pick up the little blue pills so he could take them because he didn't want to get dope-sick. Because I was checking him into detox the next morning, I agreed. I couldn't believe what I was doing, but I did it.

The next morning we woke up and called detox centers. The first one Jim called didn't want to take him because what he was taking was prescribed by a doctor. I knew he was stalling. I sat right next to him for the next call. I told him to tell them that he wanted to de-tox. Miraculously, the next rehab told him to come in. He packed a bag, and we drove half an hour to the other side of the Island. We were told it might be a long wait. We sat in the waiting room with others who were obviously going into detox themselves.

There was an older man there whose face was sucked-in, gaunt and yellow; he was bony, and his flesh was loose and hanging. He spoke to a young man sitting across from him who looked no older than twenty-five—he was sweaty, unshaven, disheveled, overweight, and very antsy. The older man started the conversation.

"Whatcha in for?"

"Xanax. You?"

"Mostly Xanax. I went into a seizure the other day. I was at my aunt's barbeque with my family, and I just dropped to the floor, foaming at the mouth. They called an ambulance. I tried to get off it myself, but I can't. How many are you doing a day?"

"Twelve, thirteen sticks. You?"

"About eight. What happened to you?"

"I'm in the thirty-day program, but I had a seizure, too."

I watched these two men chatter about their drug addiction like they were talking about a football game.

Sitting next to them were two young women who looked to be in their twenties; they had obviously just met but were talking like they had a lot in common. One said her boyfriend was an addict and had problems but that he was "so amazing." She had never been with a guy like him before, someone she felt so comfortable with. She was there for the methadone outpatient program but refused to give up her pot. She couldn't live without her pot.

The other girl was much calmer; she barely opened her eyes, and her movements were long and drawn-out. She had dark hair and dark eyes, and other than the way she was behaving, she didn't look like an addict at all. Her voice was low and calm, and she was obviously still high on something.

Neither seemed fazed in the slightest by the fact that they were about to go into detox—both were oblivious to their own problems

Here I was sitting in a detox waiting room with my husband nodding off beside me, and I was the only clean one in the room. For the first time, I was glad to be the odd man out. We waited around most of the day, and when they finally called Jim's name to admit him, I told him good luck and good-bye and to get help. As I drove away, I saw him being escorted with his suitcase to the building across the street. The sky was a clear blue and it was one of the most beautiful days all summer, but for me, it felt like rain. It felt black and gray and cold and windy. It was a sad sight, a sad day.

Monday, July 27, 2009

Jim's been in detox for five days—the most peaceful five days I've had in a year, since all this began. I don't know if it's going to work, but at least I know where he is and I know he's safe and I know at least when he comes home, he's going to be clean. That is enough for now.

Tuesday, July 28, 2009

Jim was already sitting outside waiting for me when I arrived to pick him up. I hugged him and asked how he was. He was fifteen pounds lighter, his eyes were sunken, and he was nervous and jittery. He looked like someone coming off of crack. He was still detoxing from the Xanax, apparently one of the worst drugs to come off of. He asked me for a cigarette, and I handed him the box he left with me when he went in.

He told me all about the detox—how horrible it was, how he saw the same people come in and out within days, and how the people who were in there were so far gone and so messed up that it terrified him. His sneakers were stolen. He made sure his body was covered when he sat on anything because it was so dirty and dark in there. He didn't eat. He barely slept. Maybe this taught him a lesson, maybe this would be a wake-up call—but I'd seen him say he was never going to do drugs again so many times, his words meant nothing to me now. I took him home. Later that day he was still the same: he could barely function and couldn't talk to anyone because his anxiety level was through the roof. He had begun a course of antidepressants while inside, but it would be a while before they took effect.

When he left for detox he was swollen, his stomach was bloated and distended, he was pale and gray, and his pupils had been pinpoints for the last year. Looking at him today, I could see a glimmer of the old Jim. He had lost weight, his color was coming back, and for the first time I could look into his eyes and see his pupils adjust to the sun and the dark. He still looked horrible, but it was an improvement.

Maybe there's hope.

Chapter 3: Old Habits Die Hard—August 2009

Saturday, August 8, 2009

Last night I snooped through Jim's things. How many times did I tell myself I would never do this again? Jim was asleep, and Sage was watching a movie. I logged onto his Outlook account. Old habits die hard. I had grown used to finding out about him through spying, so this didn't feel strange at all. He had an e-mail from an adult website. He even had an account profile, opened ten months earlier. He wrote that he was "interested in meeting women for a discreet affair, to meet in the day or evening to see where the time will take us."

I went limp. I felt lightheaded and wanted to vomit, but I swallowed. My daughter was in the room. In his profile, he wrote that he used drugs recreationally and that he was into voyeurism—both true.

How can this be happening? The drugs are more than enough—now this? I woke him up and told him to meet me upstairs. Sage was still watching her movie. When I showed him the computer, he had nothing to say except he signed up so he could get free porn, the answer I had anticipated. While normally that would upset me, at this point it was the least of my worries. He began to yell, claiming he didn't see the relevance of my questioning. I said that it mattered if ten months ago he was looking to have an affair—if not morally to him, then at least for my own health. I told him that cheating can result in unwanted disease if nothing else! He denied it and yelled, leaving me helpless and stunned, as if someone had just told me I had cancer.

Sunday, August 9, 2009

I was out late last night, and I woke up early and sick, with nausea in my stomach like right before I throw up. I would rather bleed from every orifice in my body than deal with what I've been dealing with for the last year.

I went outside to smoke a cigarette (I've never smoked before—it's something I picked up recently), and he followed me out. I told him to leave me alone because I had lost whatever respect for him I had left, which wasn't much. He grabbed my arm, pulled me close to him, looked straight into my eyes, and swore on our daughter's life that he had never cheated on me and never would. He said this with such conviction. I had suspicions, but I never had any evidence. He had sworn on Sage's life before and lied, but I didn't want to think about it. I felt defeated. His answer was enough for me at the moment, but I still felt broken beyond repair. The truth is I'll probably never really know. I was starting crumble. Deep down I knew his words were just a band-aid, but they were what I needed to hear. At that moment I could not handle any more.

Wednesday, August 12, 2009

Just another day, another day to wake up, go through the motions, and entertain Sage because she's on summer vacation. I took off the whole month of August, and we were supposed to be on vacation as a family at this time. This isn't what I had planned for my summer, which could have been so beautiful in our new house, with lots of parties, barbeques and days spent relaxing on the deck overlooking the water. Instead, I'm waking up every morning in my own private hell.

Friday, August 14, 2009

I can't even look at him anymore. He's made it clear that he has no tolerance for me. Six months ago Jim convinced my father to invest some of his retirement money into flipping foreclosure properties with him. Jim said he would get 100% on his return in three months. I simply mentioned the money he owes my father—more than $50,000—and he became livid, yelling at me in front of Sage. She said, "I wish you and Daddy never met!"

This is getting out of control. I confronted him after she fell asleep, and he had nothing but anger toward me. I should have expected that. I don't know why I keep getting caught in the same trap; I don't know why I keep setting myself up.

He actually told me to start acting like an adult in front of our daughter. Where does he get off? He calls me a "fucking bitch" in front of her and walks away, and that's okay? He drives high with her in the car, and he's telling me what to do? I really don't know what to do anymore.

He stormed out and said he was going to a hotel for the weekend. My parents took Sage. I called him at ten o'clock on Sunday morning to let him know what time we were supposed to pick her up, and he didn't answer. That's not like him, even high. He never gets up that late. I called the hotel, and they asked me which room I wanted—he had two under his name. Both rooms were under Jim's credit card.

Sometimes I look at myself in the mirror and ask what I did to deserve this. I don't want to play the martyr role; I genuinely don't. I cook him wonderful meals, keep the house meticulously clean, pay the bills, and take care of our daughter better than most mothers I know; I'm educated and love to work; I'm always available for sex, I keep myself in great shape, and I try so hard to love him. Why isn't that enough?

Why do I still seek his approval?

Saturday, August 22, 2009

We had a decent day today. We went out for dinner last night with Sage, and it was nice. Sad, but nice. We went for a drive, and he played me some songs by a band called Staind that he said exemplify how he feels:

Believe in me
I know you've waited for so long
Believe in me
Sometimes the weak become the strong

The words are nice, but they don't change anything. Again, I feel like I'm the only one in the relationship we had. I cry and tell him how much he's hurt me, hurt our family, and all I get back is that I have a problem and I did this to myself and I have to live with it. Call me crazy, but I expected better. I don't know why, but I did.

Sunday, August 23, 2009

This is just another night of many with no sleep, no peace, and no sanity. Jim went out again. He's barely out of detox, but he's been going out almost every weekend. This doesn't sit right with me—it makes me feel like he's not serious about his recovery. I'm starting to think his detox was a joke to him. He said he'd be with friends, but a girl kept calling the house phone. She's a friend from childhood, but I still don't think it's appropriate because she's single and obviously interested in him. She says she's "single" on Facebook.

I couldn't sleep, so I texted him at 2:30 a.m. to see if he was coming home. He texted back, "No," and that was it. I called a few times and texted again, but he didn't respond. My gut knew what he was doing. I finally got him on the phone at three thirty.

"What the fuck is going on?" he said. "I saw my friend tonight and asked her if she called the house, and she said no. I checked her phone and saw that *you* called *her*. You're acting crazy!"

"Jim, I called her back after she called the house and hung up, and then she called back again at eleven. What are you doing?"

"I'm just trying to have a good time! What's your problem?"

"Are you coming home? Sage expects to see you when she wakes up."

"Are you kidding me? Come home to you? I'm staying at a hotel."

"I won't fight with you! Just come home, please. Don't do anything stupid. Just come home, and I won't argue with you."

"Yes, you will."

"Jim, I won't. I just want you to be safe. Just come home."

"I'll think about it …" He hung up the phone.

I called back now, panicked that he was high. I went straight to the computer in a panic. I logged on to our cell phone account where I could view his phone calls up-to-the-minute. I checked his phone records and found he was calling Atlantic City and Fred, a big-time cokehead friend of his. I called the hotel where he had said he was staying, and they said they had no guests under that name. I called a hotel in Atlantic City, and they did have him checked into a room. I left him a message saying I knew where he was and what he was doing.

I didn't hear from him again until he was on his way home at noon the next day. I was with my friend Michelle when I got the call. He said I was insane and that he had just gotten a room for Fred in Atlantic City, that he was at the hotel he went to a few weekends earlier. Michelle called the hotel in front of me, and they said he was not a guest there last night, but they remembered them from the weekend before. (*Them?*)

Jim, as usual, denied everything.

Michelle's husband has known Jim for a long time, which is how I met her. We've done a lot together as couples over the years, and she knew Jim had a drug problem but she had never seen it. When he called, I let her answer the phone; he shouted and cursed at her, thinking she was me. She finally saw how he was treating me—she was in shock.

I came home hours later, and Jim was here and he showed me the charge on his card for the hotel. He said I was crazy thinking he would go to Atlantic City—didn't I know he couldn't be around places like that anymore? I had nothing to say. The credit card statement didn't lie. But I know what my gut was telling me, and I know I was right. I know he was there and I know he was high, but I can't prove it.

I don't have the energy to argue anymore.

Monday, August 24, 2009

Jim and I went out to dinner with Sage and came home to watch a movie called *The Secret.* I really liked it. What they were saying made sense: if you think about something, it will happen. When we think about what's going wrong in our lives or what we don't want, that's often what we end up getting. I thought about this a lot.

The year Jim and I lived in Manhattan, I was in school for holistic nutrition. That year I was focused on a lot of positive things: new learning I loved, new friends, a new environment, and much more. I was so busy being positive and happy that it was all I had on my mind. I stopped worrying about Jim and what he was doing, and we got along much better. I decided not to check up on everything he was telling me and to leave him alone. It was the best time of my life with my husband and my daughter—but you can't live in a fantasy world forever.

When we got home from dinner, we watched the movie together in our bed. Jim fell asleep pretty quickly, but I was restless and ovulating, which is never a good combination. We hadn't slept together since before this all started, and I guess I was lonely and needy and missed him. He was asleep in the bed, a place now where we never came close to one another. I touched his arm, just caressed it a bit. I wanted him to wake up. I wanted to be with him. I just wanted him near me. He put his arm around me, and it felt good. I felt as if nothing had happened and here I was lying with the man I loved, the man I married. I continued to stroke his arm and gently drew his hand to my breast. He responded and started stroking me, caressing me. He turned me over and undressed us both.

Everything I had been angry with him for just melted away as he lay on top of me. I was shaking; he was shaking. We were one for a moment, and then it was over. I just lay there with him still on top of me. He rolled over and held me tight, and we fell asleep. When I woke up I knew I had just made things more confusing but I was not confused about one thing—I knew that I had just made a huge mistake.

But I was confused. Why did I let the man
who just burned me, inside of me?

Thursday, August 27, 2009

I spent Wednesday enrolling for school in a registered dietician program at Brooklyn College. I couldn't eat because I was getting a colonoscopy today. But fasting didn't bother me; I've become used to it these past few months. The sick feeling in my stomach has become almost a comfort. It's the only sensation that at least makes me feel alive.

My doctor says I have irritable bowel syndrome and a spastic colon. I controlled this with diet for more than six years and hadn't had any episodes until now. I counsel clients on how to control and heal this chronic condition through lifestyle and dietary changes, and here I am suffering from it again. I feel like a fraud. Stress is taking its toll on my body. I've allowed Jim's sickness and addiction to hurt me not just emotionally, but physically now, too.

I can't let this happen anymore.

Sage and I went to my little cousin's sixth birthday party this afternoon, where all the other mothers and fathers were with their children, loving them, protecting them. I felt empty, like I was only half a family. I felt like Sage and I were robbed of a real life. Then I stopped feeling sorry for myself and realized that at least I'm not missing out on my daughter's life. Jim has missed most of it, and he'll continue to do so for as long as he keeps fooling himself. But I am here: alive, clean, and present for her through all of her moments, big and small.

Friday, August 28, 2009

Jim's going to an outpatient program at the YMCA, and I'm going to the family group to help me cope. He tested positive for Xanax, and his doctor gave him a note because he claimed that another (non-narcotic) medication he was on for his back was causing a false-positive and he had to be tested another way to prove it wasn't Xanax.

I am so sick of his bullshit.

From: Amanda
Date: Friday, August 28, 2009 10:37 AM
To: Jim
Subject: Drug Testing …

I don't want to hear your excuses or the reasons why you get the drug test. That's your business. My only concern is the results. Whether you're on drugs or not is your business. I just need to see a negative test so you can be with our daughter.

This isn't personal. I'm not mad at you or punishing you; I'm just living up to our agreement, and there are no contingencies or excuses when it comes to the safety of our daughter. From now on, if you don't have a negative test result, then you can't be alone with Sage. It's that simple.

I hope you understand.

Amanda

Jim called and said he agreed with me 100 percent. He said he took a test today and was willing to take home tests too, as long as I understood they would probably come up false-positive for the Xanax. I was relieved. Why, I don't know. I still had a bad feeling in my gut, but I went through the next few hours with a weight lifted off my shoulders. It's sad that what makes me happy now is my husband's willingness to pee in a cup, but that's what my life has become.

Tonight I'm home with Sage. She's throwing up and running a fever. I texted Jim that she was sick, and he said he'd just go out to dinner and try and get home right after. Why do I still feel disappointed about this? Why did I expect that he would actually be concerned enough to come home and check on his daughter? Everyone's telling me I just have to let it go, let him be. Sound advice, I suppose.

Jim is out, and I'm not really sure where. He said he was going to a meeting with a detox group and then out to dinner with some friends, but I'll never really know. I checked his cell-phone records to see if he was actually doing what he said. It didn't look good, but at least I didn't freak out. I didn't answer his call to the house, and I didn't try to tell him he should be home. It was a small triumph for me. He's damaged, and I cannot and will no longer try to make him better. I can only work on me.

Sage is lying next to me—sick, feverish. But I'm here. Only me, but it's enough. It has to be enough.

At least I hope it is.

Saturday, August 29, 2009

Poor Sage, she's too sick to go to her best friend's party. She's not throwing up anymore, but she still has a fever. I feel bad for her—I can't stand it when she's sick. I don't like to leave her side. She's so sweet when she's sick—no complaining at all. I love this child more than anything else in this world. I would do anything to make her happy, to shield her from all of this.

Jim got home after midnight, smelling of alcohol. He brought suppositories because Sage's fever was getting higher and I was getting nervous. I didn't believe he went where he said he did, his breath was tainted with the smell of alcohol and this morning I found a receipt on the floor of his car for parking in Atlantic City. I felt sick again.

I ran upstairs, took a deep breath, and calmly asked him if we could afford gambling when I barely have enough money to pay the bills. He denied it as usual, and I begged him to not lie to me anymore, saying it would only create an environment of mistrust. He finally admitted he went there to check a business associate in under his comps at the casino, and that he made money for it. He said he was home the same day, but I still don't believe that he was being honest. He got angry.

"It's none of your fucking business," he yelled. "I don't have to tell you everything. You're leaving me. What the fuck do you care?"

"I don't," I said. "That's the problem. I don't understand why you would lie to me. And lower your voice—our daughter can hear you!"

"You're insane, checking up on me. Worry about yourself!" he yelled and stomped out of the room.

"It's time for a drug test. Your anger is ridiculous."

He shoved a $100 bill in my hand. "Here. Go buy two tests. Your only job is to get the results of my piss, and then leave me the fuck alone."

I drove to the pharmacy. My stomach tightened, and my heart pounded so loudly I thought it was going to break through my ribs. I walked in with a knot in my throat. I bought two tests for everything but benzodiazepines (Xanax) because I knew they might come up positive. I drove home, half dreading and half eager to get this over with.

I walked up the stairs, checked on Sage, kissed her forehead, and followed Jim into the bathroom. He handed me his sample, and I took it with shaking hands. I turned the plastic cup on its side. The test strip on top started to get wet. Two lines meant negative and one line meant positive for each drug.

I had done this test many, many times before. Every time I did it, it came up positive for something. This was followed by arguing, denial, and rants about how this is a false positive and I need to send it to the lab, followed by weeks of agony, followed by results still positive.

I stood holding the box in my hand, with Jim sitting below me. He saw the box shaking violently in my hand and said I was more nervous than he was.

I knelt down. It was time to see the results. A flood of relief washed over me. All the lines were there, not one positive. My hand, still shaking, dropped the box, and tears welled up in my eyes. I grabbed Jim and hugged him tight. As much as he was the one causing the pain, he had also been a source of comfort. It was difficult to feel hurt by the person who's also the person I turn to when I'm hurt. We squeezed each other tight, and he let go and laughed. There was a brief sense of relief between us for the first time in a long time.

I love him. I hate him.

Monday, August 31, 2009

I took Sage to the Y to join a program called Little Steps, which gives children skills to cope with an addict in the family. Sage is probably holding a lot in and blaming herself. She's been exhibiting odd behavior lately, acting out a lot and always having to pee. She's suffering, and I can see it. I try to talk to her about what's going on. I ask if she's okay, but she doesn't really want to talk about it. It turns out she knows a lot more than she let on.

The counselor started off by asking her some questions.

"Hi, sweetie. I'm going to ask you some questions, and I want you to answer them the best you can, okay? How do you get along with your mom?"

"My mom? I love my mom."

"Do you have a good time with her? Do you fight?"

"No, I have fun with my mom. She plays with me."

"How about your dad? How do you get along with him?"

"Umm … okay. Good. Okay."

"Do you have fun with your dad? Do you fight with him?"

"No, sometimes we have fun."

"What do you do with your dad?"

"We have a secret from Mommy. Daddy buys me pool toys, but we don't tell Mommy because she'll get mad."

"How do Mommy and Daddy get along?"

"They fight. They fight all the time."

"What do you do when they fight?"

"I go in my toy room so I don't hear anything, and I play. They fight in the kitchen."

"How do you feel when they fight? Are you sad, angry, mad, upset, happy?"

"Mad. I get mad."

"It's normal to get mad. That's okay. Do you think anyone in your family is struggling?"

"Yes!" she said. "My dad! My dad!" She practically jumped out of her chair to answer.

"Why do you think that, honey?"

"Well, he sleeps a lot. He doesn't play with me so much."

"We help kids here deal with parents that are struggling with drugs and alcohol. Have you ever seen your dad do anything like that?"

"Yes."

"What did you see, honey?"

"I see him smoke. He smokes all the time. Cigarettes."

"Anything else?"

"I see him drink wine."

"Okay, so how do you know that he's struggling?"

"I just know. I can see it."

"Good, sweetie. We're here to help you understand what your dad is going through and to help you when you get mad or sad. We color and have a lot of fun with other kids."

The whole time, Sage spoke out of only one side of her mouth. She was squirming in the chair. She looked uncomfortable talking about this, but I was glad to hear her at least get it out. It upset me to learn she had been holding it in. As she spoke about her dad, tears dripped slowly down my cheeks.

How could I have chosen this man as her father?

His daughter loves riding horses at five years old. She loves nature: dinosaurs, digging, collecting rocks, animals, swimming, and so many other wonderful things. She's intelligent, sensitive, sweet, caring, beautiful, loving, trusting, playful, funny, and talented.

Doesn't he care?

Chapter 4: No Sleep— September 2009

Wednesday, September 2, 2009

Today I took Sage to the Botanical Gardens with her best friend Lilly and her mother, seven months pregnant with her third child. Her husband had been a drug addict as well, and we bonded over how similar our experiences were. He had lied and manipulated like Jim, but he'd been mostly clean since Lilly was born. He still smoked pot and drank, but she seemed okay with it. I was envious. This should be me. I should be having more children and having a normal life with Jim. Why couldn't he stay straight?

My best friend Jackie was home for two weeks from medical school, and she came over when Jim was having one of his better days. He was in the kitchen with us acting normal, funny and charming. We were cooking dinner together like we used to, as if nothing had changed between us. One of us would pick up cooking where the other left off, and we always ended up with a beautiful meal. I kept thinking to myself that this is what life should be like with him, that this is the man I married. Jackie had told me I should divorce Jim a long time ago. She knew everything, and she knew he wasn't going to change. She had the foresight I had blinded myself to a long time ago. But after seeing him that day, she called me and said she felt bad.

She could see he really did want to be a better person, and she really did wish there were a way to work things out because, after all, we were a family. She suggested I just leave him alone and see if he could get it together. For a moment I had a glimmer of hope. If Jackie can see that there's some good in him, then maybe I've been right all along. Maybe he can get better.

Maybe there is hope.

Saturday, September 5, 2009

Last night Jim went out again. He said he was going to an NA meeting and that he'd be home early because he was going to watch Sage the next day. I had to cater a party, and then I was going out.

He said he'd be home by ten o'clock; then he texted around nine thirty to say it would probably be closer to midnight, but not to worry because he was looking forward to a fun day with Sage. I didn't get upset, but I couldn't sleep.

Midnight turned to one o'clock, two o'clock, and then three o'clock. Finally at 5:15 a.m., I texted just to see if he was still alive. He texted back that he was sorry he had worried me, but he'd be home in fifteen minutes and it had been a sad night.

I gave him the benefit of the doubt, but as soon as he staggered in, super-sized cup of coffee in hand, smell of stale cigarettes and alcohol on his breath, I could see he was high. He was slurring words, and his eyes were off, glazed over and blank. He blamed it on no sleep and the five cups of coffee he said he drank over the last few hours.

I don't know why I even entertained the story he was about to tell me; it was like being in the mind of a madman. He said he might have saved someone's life. He said he was at an NA meeting and that (here the details of the story changed a few times) he got a call from Fred saying his brother was out of control on angel dust. He said he spent the night trying to find him and that he called someone from NA to help get him into a detox unit. He said he had spent the last four hours at the hospital, but when I looked at his phone, it showed texts back and forth with Fred's brother until 3:30 a.m. They were going to meet up, and he wanted Jim to "do another bump" (a line of coke) and get a drink with him. Jim's texts back were "Yup" and "I'll come find you." He changed his story a couple more times: first he went to Brooklyn to find the brother, then Fred was with him, then not with him, practically in the same breath. What I got from the story was that he went out with Fred's brother, they drank and did some coke, and then Fred's brother got out of control and Jim called Fred to help take him to the hospital. Here he was, stoned to the gills, and he looked proud of himself.

He was swaying back and forth, and looked pretty calm for someone who just drank five cups of coffee.

I asked him to take a urine test, and he said absolutely. "No problem. I'm not on anything. I figured you'd have one waiting for me."

Somehow, after all that coffee, a large bottle of water, and two more large glasses of water, he still couldn't pee. I was crying. I hated him for doing this.

This is not how my life should be!

"What are you doing to yourself?" I cried. "What are you doing to us?"

"What are you crying about? Please! Would you be quiet?"

I couldn't. I held myself wrapped up like a ball, rocking back and forth.

He said he'd be fine taking care of Sage, and I told him he wouldn't be taking care of anybody until he took a drug test that came up negative. He said he still couldn't pee and went to sleep. I was so sick of the games. I had to ask my dad to come over because Jim was useless on the basement couch, snoring and dead to the world around him as Sage ran in and out of the basement with my father to use the pool. Jim didn't stir.

I had to leave for work soon, and I didn't want to go without giving him a test; if I did, he'd wake up and pee, and I wouldn't be there. I asked him to take the test, and he said no, that he was still exhausted.

"Then I'll assume it's positive. You won't be able to be alone with Sage."

"I'll take it when I get up. Just get the fuck out of here."

"It's your call."

He reluctantly followed me upstairs. I put the test strip in the cup, and he immediately came up positive for cocaine. The same lump in my throat formed, the pounding of my heart became violent, and I felt sick to my stomach. This test wasn't for Xanax, which I'm sure he took before he came home because he was so calm.

He said to wait ten minutes and the line would come up. I said I was pretty sure it was accurate, but fine, we could wait. Ten minutes passed, and of course it was still positive.

"Jesus, Jim. You're barely six weeks clean. What are you doing?"

"It's wrong. If I was on coke, would I come home? I was helping somebody. I was a hero last night. Send it to the lab and you'll see."

"It's not wrong. You are no longer allowed to see our daughter unsupervised. What's wrong with you? We agreed on this!"

He glared at me and turned furious. "You fucking bitch. Don't you *ever* tell me I can't see my daughter! I'll see her whenever I want." He lunged at me, and I moved out of his way. He shot past me and slammed the door so hard behind him it sounded like it cracked. I just stood there, afraid of him—afraid of the drugs and who he became when he was on them. He went outside to smoke a cigarette, and the phone rang.

It was his mom. I told her what had happened and started sobbing. She told me to be strong for Sage.

Jim's too far gone, and my only concern now is keeping Sage safe.

I couldn't breathe. It literally felt as if he had kicked me in the stomach; I wanted to throw up. I wanted to fall down. I couldn't stop crying and shaking.

Jim came back in, walked past me without even a glance in my direction, and started his shower routine. I had to have him understand that he could not be on drugs around our daughter, and I told him so again, through the steam of the shower, very calmly this time. All he could say was, "Bring the test to the lab and you'll see." He seems to think that if he can buy himself a little time, things will go away.

I wish I could go away, too.

I took the food to my client's party and tried to keep my visit quick and the conversation light. Small talk was something I was getting good at—if someone got too close, I wouldn't be able to control myself. The tears came out so naturally, I couldn't stop them.

Afterward I bought a pack of cigarettes, smoked until I felt sick, and then headed to the post office to send Jim's urine to the lab. It was closed, so I went home. My dad had taken Sage out, and Jim had gone to the store—or at least that's what he'd said. He was gone for more than an hour, though, so I assumed he went to get more Xanax so he could sleep off the coke.

I don't think I was far off, because he was practically in a coma until I woke him at seven thirty that evening. I told him Sage was going to bed and that I was really disappointed, because what would I have done without my parents today? He had been completely out of it—what if they weren't around? I just didn't understand his lack of remorse for how he was treating Sage. Why wasn't Sage a priority for him? Wasn't it important to keep his word to her? As a little boy, he used to spend weekends with his own dad, who would leave him all alone or be too drugged-up to talk to, and it scared him. Now he's doing it to his own daughter. I guess it seems okay to him because there's always someone around to take up his slack.

"Well," he said, "it didn't work out that I could watch her."

That was his answer, that "it" didn't "work out."

I just didn't understand.

I'm not a believer in the conventional version of God, but I think I may finally understand what people mean by "Let go and let God." Let him go, and God will take care of me. Have I had a God complex all this time? Did I really think I could save him from himself, from the drugs? If I can let him go, then maybe at least I can save myself.

Maybe at least I can save Sage.

Sunday, September 6, 2009

I knew Jim was awake because I could hear his smoker's cough. He hadn't even bothered to come upstairs to say good morning to his daughter, and he'd been up for at least an hour. Sage knew he was in the basement, and she hadn't even asked about him.

I got in the shower and started to wash. I sat on the bench and began to scrub my legs. I'm wasting away. My legs look bony, and my stomach is so emaciated that my ribs, which have always been visible, are now gauntly protruding. My mind is sick, and my body is getting sick, too.

I dropped Sage off at Jim's mother's house, and something finally started to click in my head. I had just been saying it before, but now I was starting to truly understand it: Jim isn't Jim anymore. I have to forget the man I've been trying to reach for so long, the man who comes out in little bits and pieces. Jim isn't Jim. The drugs and the mentality of drug addiction are all he is now. It would take years for him to again become the man I love. But he may never have been who I thought he was in the first place. It's the good moments that addicts show us—because they're not all bad—that keep us hanging on long after we should say good-bye.

I also was angry because even though Jim is no longer Jim, before this started he had to make a choice, and he chose lies and drugs over his wife and daughter. I would have gone to hell and back for him if only he would have been honest with me. He never was.

He really never was.

I'm beginning to understand why addiction is called a disease. He really is sick, beyond help at this point. This disease festers, it eats away at people slowly—and it doesn't stop at just one victim. It's eating away at my strength, my mind, my sanity, forcing its way into my body and making it sick, too.

Jim is fooling himself. He's on his own, and he has been for a long time. His agreement to go to detox was halfhearted. He wanted to get help, but he wasn't really ready. He needs to hit a bottom that I can't warn him about—he needs to actually experience it. I've already hit my bottom. My two biggest fears now are how this will affect our daughter in the future, and that Jim's bottom will be death. Maybe soon, and maybe years from now. Either way, Sage and I will have to deal with it one day.

When I got home, Jim was there, showered and dressed and looking totally normal. Maybe he slept it off. I thought he would finally want to spend some time with Sage, and he did go out back for a few minutes to hunt rocks with her, but then he said he had to go to the pharmacy and had errands to run.

I was exhausted and hoped he could spend the rest of the night with her so I could have a break. He said he was sorry, but he had already made plans.

"Don't worry—they're not with a woman."

"If you're going to stay out all night and sleep all day, then tell me now. I don't want you to disappoint her again."

He picked up his keys. "I'll be home early."

"You've said that before."

"Whatever. I have to go."

My mom called from my Aunt Rachel's house and said to come by with Sage. I jumped at the chance. I couldn't bear another sleepless night worrying over whether Jim was going to come home high, or at all. We talked until late, and it was good to have supportive people around me. I listened to my family tell me I would be fine. They knew I was a great person and I would be happy again soon. I could hear the words but the meaning would not sink in. I was still so shaken that my stomach was upset. I ate dinner, but I couldn't keep anything down. My body was rejecting nourishment.

Nothing would penetrate.

I decided to sleep over at my mom's house. When I stopped home to pick up some clothes at 10:30 p.m., Jim still wasn't home. I didn't think he'd be there, but I had hoped he would. I turned my cell phone off. The less I knew at this point, the better. Let go and let God.

Sage said to me after Jim left, "Mommy, we got so many rocks—we did Team Sage and Daddy!" She sounded so proud of what she and her father had done together.

"I wish we could have gotten more, but Daddy had to go."

"Baby, remember how I said Daddy is sick? He's just not okay right now, and although he may do some strange things, he loves you, baby."

"I know, I know. Let's go, Mommy. I want to go now."

It took every bit of energy in me not to start crying. Maybe one day I can forgive him for what he's done to me, but I don't think I'll ever be able to forgive him for what he's doing to our daughter. I knew when I looked into her eyes and saw how happy she was to have ten quality minutes with her dad that I could never forgive him.

Monday, September 7, 2009—Labor Day

Today was a day I will never forget. I didn't think things could get any worse. Most families were barbequing and celebrating the end of summer; we should have been, too. I woke up with Sage at my mother's house and planned to go to breakfast with my friend Michelle. Before I went to meet her, around eleven thirty, Jim finally called. (He had called the night before while I was sleeping—at about one thirty in the morning—to ask if Sage was all right.) I answered the phone, dreading the person I knew I had to speak to.

"Where are you? Where is our daughter?"

"She's fine. We stayed at my mother's."

"I was going to spend the day with her, remember?"

"Jim, it's eleven thirty. Why didn't you call earlier?"

"I left you a message last night, and I never heard back from you."

"Do you want to see her? I'll bring her home in an hour."

"Fine."

That was all. He hung up before I could speak another word.

An hour later, I walked in the door with Sage, and as soon as I looked at him, I could see everything I needed to know. His complexion was chalky, his stomach was bloated, and he could barely breathe through his nose. The edges of his nostrils were bright red. I just looked at him, half in sadness and half in disgust.

"What? What are you looking at?" he demanded.

"You used last night. Look at your nose."

"I've been stuffy for a month. It's allergies. Please, Amanda. Just wait until the test results come back."

"All I have to do is look at you. You look like hell. Where were you?"

"I was at the Yellow Fin until twelve, and then I went home. I was with this guy Mike from NA—you can check my phone. I'm going to a meeting with him tonight. I think I'm going to ask him to be my sponsor."

"Jim, I know all I need to know by looking at you."

He couldn't look back at me. He didn't have to say another word.

I still decided to give Sage time to look for rocks and swim with him while I was home. While they were together, something told me to look in his car. It was just an intuition. With my heart pounding, I snuck into the garage and lifted the trunk as delicately as I could. Almost instantly I found a small bag of cocaine. I called Jim's mother, and she told me to get Sage and leave the house.

Before Jim went to detox, he told me he had been in some trouble, and was working with a government agent on a big case as a witness. I was told I was not allowed to say anything about it, but I still wasn't sure if this was real or fake, fantasy or reality. Either way I was frightened. This man had been calling me to ask about Jim, so now I had a reason to call him. He answered immediately and read me my rights. He told me that if I lied, I would be arrested. I was terrified, to put it mildly. I told him what I had found and asked him what I needed to do. I was shaking and sweating. I was freezing and on fire at the same time. He said I should bring the bag of cocaine to him. So be it: I wasn't going to keep secrets anymore. If Jim wanted to do this, he had to pay the consequences. Secretly I hoped that this agent would help me help Jim. I hoped he would make Jim get help.

Jim walked in with Sage, and I immediately went ahead with the plan to get out of there fast. He seemed almost relieved that we were leaving. Shaking, short of breath, dizzy, and scared, I got us out of there quickly. I went to his mom's house and showed her the bag of coke. She barely glanced at it. I told her what I needed to do.

Jim called and warned me that the man from the government was coming over to talk to him. We took Sage and her cousin to eat, and I couldn't even look at food; the smell made me nauseous. I got a call from the agent, asking if I knew where Jim was because he wasn't answering his phone and they were supposed to meet. He said to meet him with the drugs in a parking lot.

I was trembling when he pulled up. He got into my car and just sat there. I said jokingly, "I don't smoke, but I just started. You want one?"

He said, "Those'll kill you, you know."

I half smiled and said, "I know."

We went over everything: where I found the drugs, who Jim was doing them with, and I told him about Fred and his brother. I asked him if I was doing the right thing, if I was making a mistake. He said of course I wasn't. I said, "Please, just get him help. Make him stop this." In the past, I would have lied through my teeth for him, even if it meant risking my own freedom. But not anymore, not this time.

I didn't want to be involved with the trouble Jim was in, and I was willing to tell the truth no matter the consequences. He wasn't worried about me or our daughter. He didn't give a second thought to getting behind the wheel with her in the car when he was on all kinds of pills. He needed more help than I could give him. They say, "The truth shall set you free." I was willing to tell the truth if it would set me free from Jim.

The agent said he had been calling Jim and that he even stopped by our house, but that nobody answered the door. I said he was probably out cold. I asked him what he could do, and he said not much except try to get the truth out of Jim. But Jim is a vault about drugs, even when you catch him red-handed.

We went to the house together, and sure enough, he was passed out on the couch in the fetal position. He didn't wake for any noise. The man looked at me and shook his head as if he had seen this a million times. "Jesus," he gasped under his breath. I nudged Jim, and he jumped up.

I left them to speak in private, and called Jim's friend Meg. He had said to call if I ever needed help, and I needed it now. I asked him to please intervene between Jim and Fred and his brother, to please tell them to stay away. He said of course, but that first he would talk to Jim, to tell him to stop this.

"Meg, you know you can't stop him. You know he won't stop. He's so far gone now. He's been high all weekend, and he plans to go out again tonight. He's going to die. He's not going to stop until he kills himself."

"I'll talk to him."

I left while the agent was still speaking to Jim, and went back to get Sage at my mother-in-laws' house and figure out what to do next.

Later on, Jim called, asking what had happened to Sage and why wasn't I bringing her back like I had promised earlier. He had no knowledge of what I just did with the agent.

"Jim, you know why. You were out doing coke all night. I don't want her to see that—we agreed on this."

"I was not, Amanda! I got home at midnight!"

"Jim, I found it."

He said, of course, that it wasn't his. I hung up.

Within seconds, I got a call from the agent.

"What happened?" I asked.

"Not much. He admitted some things and not others."

"But couldn't you see, didn't you see him? Didn't you look at his nose? He was just using. What do I do now?"

"Send the test to the lab, and when you get the results back, we can see. Then I can confront him."

"In the meantime, I just watch him get high in front of our daughter?"

"This is a serious accusation."

"Test him yourself right now and you'll see! Can't you do anything?"

"He has to want to get help. If he doesn't, we can't work with him."

My mother-in-law and I took the kids to the park, and I got another call from Jim.

"So, you're just going to take our daughter from house to house like a vagabond? You're gonna just not come home?"

"Jim, she's safe. That's all that matters. Go look in the mirror—do you want her to see you like that?"

"She didn't see anything. I was fine when I saw her."

"Jim, please. You said if this ever happened again not to let her see you like that. 'Run away,' you said. 'Take her and go.' That's what I'm doing. Please get help."

Tonight, as I put her to bed, Sage said, "Daddy and I were looking for rocks, and Daddy slipped and almost fell down the hill. I almost fell down the hill, too. Mommy, you know Daddy looked like a gray ghost. He looked gray. Did you see that, Mommy?"

I almost lost it, but I kept my composure and spoke about it sweetly, telling her that her daddy was sick and one day we hoped that he would stop doing bad things and get better. She drifted off to sleep holding onto me. I walked down the stairs and cried.

I cried for Sage, for what her own father was making her go through, and I cried for my husband, the man I was watching slowly self-destruct, the loneliest soul I had ever known. I cried because he would never know the loveliest little soul I had ever known. I texted him a picture of Sage and him laughing, and I turned off my phone.

Tuesday, September 8, 2009

I slept a total of three hours last night and came home to shower and asked Jim about an SUV we had leased in my name. He said it was in the shop, but it's been gone for three weeks now. The minute I saw him, I could see he had not only been out the night before, but he was still high. He hadn't slept, and he was fueled with anger. For the first time ever, I was actually afraid of him doing more than just shoving me. He had never been violent when he was not high. He had a temper but I never feared he would really hurt me. This new Jim was inhuman and unpredictable. He looked like he wanted to hurt someone, anyone, and I was not exempt from his rage. It seemed, in the last few months, that I was always on the receiving end of it. I was shaking. I didn't think I could take any more. I should have known what would happen next.

I called the shop where Jim said the SUV was at, in front of him, and was told it wasn't there. Jim started yelling, "It's there!" His friend at the shop told me he was sorry for this mess. He knew Jim was using him in his lies and he had told Jim to give the car back to me. He also told me he assumed Jim was on drugs again because he knew him in the past. I sadly confirmed it was true.

I hung up the phone and calmly asked Jim who had the car and said I would handle getting it back from here. He said I couldn't handle who had it. (*Was he quoting movies now?*) I said if it didn't come back, I was going to report it stolen.

"If you do that, I will fucking leave here and give you nothing. I pay the goddamn bills here."

"I just want it back."

"Go ahead and report it stolen—see what happens."

"I just spoke to the shop, and they say they never had it. What do you want me to do?"

"Shut the fuck up. I'll have it back tonight. After that, you pay for it. Just shut up and get the fuck out of here."

I started to cry, and he dismissed my tears with more rage, throwing his chair to the floor and cursing, shouting at me. I walked away crying and went upstairs to shower. I saw the laundry basket was full. I started separating the clothes. On three hours of sleep, shaking like a leaf and crying, I went through his pants pockets. Full of Xanax. He clearly hadn't taken any yet to come down off the coke because he wouldn't be this brutal except when he was high on coke.

I knew Sage would have to come home later. I didn't have the energy to move her around tonight. I wanted peace, and I didn't know when he would stop. I'm not proud of what I did next—it was like someone else took over.

I took one two-milligram stick of Xanax and left the rest. I crushed it and put the powder in a square of tin foil and went downstairs. I told Jim I was going out for a bagel and coffee and asked if he wanted anything, ever the good wife. He said to pick him up the same—he didn't even look up from the TV he was staring blankly at. I went to the store and bought two plain bagels and coffee.

I kept hearing his voice in my head, telling me to "shut up and get the fuck out of here." I spread butter on his bagel and mixed in the white powder. "Go ahead and report it stolen—see what happens," I heard his voice again, "I will leave you with nothing." I put the bagel back together and cut it in half. I placed the bagel on a plate and walked toward the stairs. I knew that when he took Xanax, he took much more than this, so I knew it might not even affect him, but I wanted him to be calm. I wanted him to stop. I needed him to stop.

I walked down the stairs and handed him the bagel. I watched him as he ate. Within an hour, he was asleep on the couch. He was a different person, and now so was I.

Friday, September 11, 2009

This is a sad day for many people, and it's a sad day for me, too. Every day is a sad day for me. I'm looking for the light at the end of the tunnel, and the wind keeps blowing out my candle along the way.

I've long suspected that Jim hasn't been honest about our finances.

Money, it seemed, was always available, and he supported us in a very nice lifestyle, so I never knew how bad things really were. It seems now we're practically in financial ruin, in fact I do not think we were ever financially okay. The last building he bought for development has been on hold for three years. It's sucked us dry financially, and he's been borrowing millions of dollars to keep the deal afloat. I knew some of it, but I never knew the full story, which was the way he liked it. It appears that he's not just a drug addict, but a fraud as well.

The $50,000 Jim borrowed from my father he still hasn't paid back. My father is retired, and that's a lot of money for him. Jim said he was flipping some foreclosure properties and that he'd have the money back, plus 100 percent more, in three months; that was seven months ago. I don't think there ever really was a deal. Jim still insists, and says every week that he'll have the money.

He's stopped giving me checks to cover household expenses. It's been months. He gives me a little cash here and there for bills, but that's it. Where he gets the cash from I cannot even begin to imagine. Financial trouble would never have bothered me if I'd known about it—I would have worked full-time, take on a second job!—but he kept it from me. In my work as a Health Coach I was never concerned with how much money I made. I loved to help people and worked only part-time so I could be home with Sage. I believed I didn't need the money. I was naïve, and I trusted him completely. He said things were going to work out, that he had everything under control. But things are not under control. He has people accosting him every day, asking for their money. We're broke. Everything Jim has made has gone into this Hope Street project and a lifestyle we can't afford and never could.

He hasn't done our taxes in three years, maybe more and I had no idea. He showed me a letter the other day from an accountant that said we didn't have to file because we hadn't made any money and were simply borrowing and in debt. This doesn't make sense to me. Jim told me every year that he was filing our taxes and the reason I didn't have to sign them was that he put me on as a dependent.

How could I have trusted this man?

We live in a house we were supposed to buy a year ago, and the sellers want us out because Jim hasn't paid them. We were served eviction papers back in March, but somehow he smoothed that over, saying it was a mistake.

He has lied about *everything*!

I am his wife—how could I have let him fool me for so long? If Hope Street doesn't close, I'll probably have to declare bankruptcy. I have perfect credit, but I have no money to pay the bills or either of the two car leases in my name. Jim convinced me to lease a Mercedes and Audi SUV in my name. I've never had a late payment in my life, and now I'm trying to figure out how to pay bills with nothing. I'm looking for a full-time job with benefits, but the economy is terrible; and even if I find one, it won't put a dent in our bills. Jim keeps telling me he's getting a bridge loan until the building closes, but this has been going on now for over two months.

It wouldn't be so bad if he had just come clean with me a year ago. We moved into a huge house we couldn't afford when we could have moved into a smaller one, or an apartment. I wouldn't have spent $25,000 on furniture or $8,000 to have the house painted and thousands more on little odds and ends. If we hadn't moved into this house, I could have had the money in the bank from our previous house: $50,000. I've been balancing the bills for the past month with pennies—literally down to the last cent. I've used some savings from my business account from my Health Coaching practice, but soon that will be gone, too. How could I have been so naïve?

I just had dinner with Jim and Sage, and now he's out at a meeting, or so he says. I'm worried that much like the last four weekends, he's going to stay out late and come home high. But I'm strangely calm, and I hope I stay this way. You'd think I'd be immune to all of this craziness by now. I'm not, but I think I'm growing a little stronger day by day.

My friend Madelyn wrote me an e-mail today suggesting that I kick Jim out. She doesn't think he should be allowed in the house if he's using. I agree with her, but he can't afford to leave and I can't count on him to pay the bills here if he does and most of the bills are in my name. I have to wait until he closes on the building. Once that happens, he can pay off his debt and start giving me the commercial rent as per our agreement when we go for a divorce: $15,000 a month for the rest of my life. How I pray every day that "Hope Street" isn't just another lie or fantasy. I hope Jim can keep clean long enough to actually follow through. I'm not being greedy—he's going to make much more than that. I need to secure a future for our daughter. I don't want her to want for anything.

But this building has been closing for the last two and a half years. Jim has borrowed so much money and burned so many bridges in the meantime that I just don't know how it can all turn out well. Friends, family, business associates—nobody takes him seriously anymore. His close friends are all pretty straight with me, and even they admit that he's an exaggerator and a bull-shitter. They are worried for the money they "invested" with Jim.

Documents on our computers show pieces of a puzzle that Jim has spread all over the place, hoping I wouldn't find them. In documents hidden on his computer there is his personal financial statement that says he's borrowed over 9 million dollars against a building he owns only a third of. His credit cards are maxed out, and he's getting late charges every month. He bounces checks to the credit card companies. I thought he was making money for us and borrowing only for building expenses—and not to the tune of 9 million dollars! We've been living on other people's money for the longest time, and I've been oblivious.

Now that I think about it, people have been hounding Jim for money as long as I've known him; he always blamed the other guy, and it didn't occur to me until recently to doubt him. When we first met, his mom was getting phone calls from a neighbor about money. Apparently they invested money with Jim for something but never saw their money again. My uncle gave him a loan for another business venture and wasn't paid back for five years. My cousin Jason gave him money to buy a house that had actually been sold to someone else; it took months for him to get the money back. Jason lent Jim money again, which he did pay back with interest, but not without a struggle and a pile of excuses. Jim always claims that people are screwing him over, or that he "didn't know." His stories are unbelievable, but he tells them with such conviction that people believe him.

Tuesday, September 15, 2009

Last night I went to a charity fundraiser, and when I got home, the phone rang. It was my dad. He had been subpoenaed to answer questions about a lawsuit against Jim that's been pending for more than three years now. He was furious, and rushed over with my mother, in pajamas. Somehow, Jim talked him down. It seems every time I try to see Jim for whom I thought he was at one time, something intervenes.

He lies; this I know. He manipulates, he deceives, and he uses. He is unhealthy. He is not a good husband, and he is not a good father. He turns to drugs instead of family. I never thought this would happen to me. I've seen the stories of women and families whose every day was a private hell. They don't know from moment to moment what their loved one will do, whether they'll use or steal or cheat or leave.

We start to live with or without things that we never imagined. I am now dealing with everything I had said was not going to happen to me. I'm starting to accept new realities and make excuses for things I would never have accepted in the past.

After Jim's relapse three years ago, I swore—to him and to myself—that if it ever happened again, I would leave him and never look back. Four months ago, when I confirmed his prescription drug use and saw his positive cocaine test, I took a step down without even realizing it. I thought, "At least he doesn't get high and stay out all night. At least he's not cheating, and he's admitting he needs help and is going for it." A step down. Then he lied to me for months, telling me he was clean when he was still getting high on prescription meds. When I found out I thought, "At least he isn't getting drugs off the street." Another step down. Then he went to detox, and I thought, "At least he's getting help; it's not like those stories you hear where the addict is in denial." Another step down. A week later, he started going out and staying at hotels, telling me he didn't want to fight, that he needed some peace. I thought, "Well, at least I know where he's been, and he's coming home the next day looking sober." Another step down. Then he started to abuse me verbally, which he had done in the past but now much more violently. I thought, "At least he's not hitting us." Another step down.

I keep reducing things until soon there will be nothing left. I'll be like the addict living on the street with no money, wondering, "How did this happen?" I stopped taking care of myself and started letting my husband's addiction rule my life, that's how. I wanted so much to repair this broken man, to make him better so he could be the husband I always wanted and the father our daughter deserves. Coming from a broken family myself, I know what it's like to make excuses and live in fear, so this feels like home.

But I don't want to live here anymore.

Thursday, September 17, 2009

I met my friend Susan while living in the city. We went to the same school for integrative nutrition and we had so much in common. She was also going through a divorce. She moved to Oregon shortly after school ended but we kept in touch often.

From: Amanda
Date: Thursday, September 17, 2009 10:07 AM
To: Susan
Subject: Life

Hi Susan,

You sound great, so spirited and positive. Congrats on all the paying clients; I knew you would do it. It sounds like getting away from John was a great step for you. You sound free.

I wish I could say things are good here, but they're not. I've been trying so hard to be positive, and I don't know when the last time we spoke was, but Jim went into a 5-day detox 6-7 weeks ago. I'm pretty sure he starting doing coke again soon after. When I tested him Labor Day weekend, he came up positive, and I found some in his car. It's been really tough for me, because when he uses, he's angry and violent and verbally abusive. I have to tell him he can't see Sage that way; when he's high he doesn't agree, but when he gets sober, he says he understands. It's like Dr. Jekyll and Mr. Hyde. The drugs have really messed him up this time, and I don't know if he'll ever fully recover. I'm trying to get things settled financially so he can afford to move out—hopefully in a few weeks or a couple of months, I'm not sure yet.

I'm journaling like crazy about what is going on, and it's really helpful. I'm thinking of turning it into a book to try and help other people who are going through this. Obviously it's not done yet—the story's still unfolding—but hopefully it will be when I am able to move on from this. It's helpful for me in the meantime.

I'm sorry to sound so sad. I don't even feel like myself anymore, and it's hard to make it through the day without crying. It's been really tough, but I'm trying to focus on the light at the end of the tunnel. I know it's there, I just can't see it yet.

Hugs,

Amanda

I took Sage to Little Steps at the Y again tonight. She actually enjoyed it. I was happy. But I saw a lot of grandparents there who had custody of their grandchildren because the parents were out of the picture or on drugs. I felt awful for those kids. I know they were lucky to have such devotion from their grandparents, but these people looked overwhelmed and exhausted. They were older and should have been enjoying their grandchildren, not raising them.

Sage is lucky to have at least one stable parent. I will always be here for her. Nothing inspires me to be whole again more than she does. I guess what I'm saying is that I'm finally seeing that being her mother is the light at the end of my tunnel. It has to be.

(I did get some useful information at the Y about how to handle going to court with someone on drugs. It's not pretty, but there are some things I can do and it seems the court takes a drug-addicted parent very seriously.)

Jim and I spoke tonight after he came home from his NA meeting. We had a long talk, and it was like talking to the old Jim, the calm and rational Jim, Dr. Jekyll. The results came back from the lab, and his urine sample was positive for cocaine.

"If you knew it was going to come back positive, why did you keep telling me to wait for the results?"

"It's not that I hoped it would come back negative. I just couldn't deal with talking to you about it right then. I needed time."

"I don't know what to do anymore. Do you realize how you treat me when you're high? You're violent, mean, and scary. This is killing me. I wake up every day with just enough energy to be a good parent for Sage, and no more. I cry all the time."

I looked at him. "We can sit here and have these heart-to-hearts, which we've done a million times, but then you go right back to lying and using. I'm watching you kill yourself, and I don't think you have any idea how that makes me feel. Every time you leave, I just pray you'll come home; I'm so relieved when I hear your car pull up. I don't know who I am anymore. I am relieved I can talk to you right now, but I know once you leave this room, I may lose you again." Tears rolled down my cheeks, and I couldn't form any more words.

"I am so sorry for what I've done to you," he said. "That's all I can say. I know I'm sick. I know I need help. I'm going to NA and connecting with people." He stared into the air a foot or two in front of his face. "I went out

Labor Day weekend, and I was really fucked up. I had a couple of drinks, got in the car with Fred, and did a few bumps. I stopped because I knew I had made a mistake. After I left them, I called someone from NA, and we talked in my car for two hours. I know I fucked up."

"There's no way you could have looked like that from a couple of lines of coke."

"You don't have to believe me."

"Jim, I feel like I'm the only person in your life who has wanted nothing from you but you. Everyone else wants something—a job, money, a favor, something. I just wanted to be with you and raise a family. But you never gave me a chance.

"I asked you to call Fred and his brother and tell them to stay away, and you said no. You don't want to insult them or confront them, but me you'll insult, deceive, curse, and abuse. You say you love me, but you treat me like I'm disposable. How is that supposed to make me feel?"

"How can you say that? The year we lived in the city was the best year of my life."

"Mine, too. But one year doesn't make up for twelve. I can't trust you. Do you know what it is like to look into your eyes and see you lie to me?"

Jim said, "It's like a switch goes off in my head, and no matter how much the lie hurts you, I can't stop. I always think the truth is worse. I know it sounds sick, but I feel like I'm protecting you."

"Listen," I said. "From now on, while you're still here, I have to protect Sage from this. I talked to the group today, and they told me how to handle the situation if you come home high." I started to get choked up, and tears were falling again. "I will call ACS, and they'll send someone here to evaluate the situation. They'll take a sample of your hair, and they can mandate you out of the house and into a treatment program. They'll give you supervised visits with Sage once a week. That's it. I don't mean to sound cold, but I won't let her see you high again, *ever*. She's just a little girl who doesn't deserve to being going through this. You're out doing drugs, and I'm raising our daughter alone. She deserves us both."

"I won't say *never*," he said, "but hopefully this will never happen again.

Last weekend it felt so great just to play with her. It was the best weekend I've had in a long time, and these last couple of mornings when she came downstairs to lie with me before school …" his voice began to quaver, "I can't tell you how that felt. I am going to be a good father for her. I will."

"I've been waiting for that for five years. I want to just hug you and take all of this away from you and make it better, but I can't."

"I know you can't, but you can still hug me."

I did.

Monday, September 21, 2009

I've begun to picture what my life might be like if I were happy. I could wake up in the morning and not have to worry about where Jim has been. I could do laundry and clean without fear of finding drugs. I wouldn't have to depend on Jim for money.

I've even pictured myself in a new relationship, which, believe it or not, is a big step for me. My past, present and future always began and ended with Jim. To even fathom a life without him was painful. Even when I broke up with him, in the back of my mind I knew we would be together again. The man I picture would be nothing like Jim. He'd be healthy, successful, honest, selfless, and clean. He'd be confident and in a good place in his life. He'd have a career he loves and good friends, and he would be completely in love with me. He'd enjoy sex and have a healthy appetite for it. He'd be there for me when I needed him and would have no need to lie. He wouldn't be perfect, but he'd be real. When he would tell me he was running out to the store or to meet a client and would be back in a few hours, I wouldn't give it a second thought; I could just believe.

This man wouldn't be weak; he wouldn't have to get high or drink to deal with his life; he'd love his life. He would show me that he cares. He would love his family.

The picture of the man I want is clear to me. I tried to make Jim into this man because I was attracted to him and his recklessness—it was all I knew. I've been involved with this sickness for so long I don't even know what it would be like to just breathe anymore, to be with someone and feel clearheaded. I want that now more than anything. I don't think I would have been ready for someone who was normal, someone healthy, unless I had been to the other side, unless I had faced it head-on. I now know that there's nothing mysterious or sexy about it at all, that it is, in fact, just darkness and shadows.

Wednesday, September 23, 2009

They say things get worse before they get better. I'm going to assume that this is the worst. At least I hope it is. Yesterday I started to cook some artichokes for Sage—one of her favorite dinners. A song came over the radio: "All at Once," by Bonnie Raitt. I remembered it from high school. I always loved it, but I didn't understand it until now. As she sang, tears began to well up in my eyes until I couldn't see what I was doing. I put down my knife and just cried.

> They say women, we're the stronger
> Somehow we always make it through
> Hell, that ain't how I feel right now
> I don't even think it's true

It's simple: I'm broken. I try to appear whole on the outside to others. I pretend I'm making it through, but if anyone looks inside me, really looks, they'll see something damaged beyond repair. I used to do all of my chores, work with clients, study, read, make dinner, exercise, and talk with friends. I never had a spare moment to relax. I was getting everything done so when I picked Sage up from school, I could be totally available to her. I was busy and optimistic.

These last couple of months after I drop her off, I barely have time to shower before I have to go get her. I go through the motions of cleaning and cooking and doing the things I have to do, but I don't have the strength to do anything else. I've let my counseling practice go, my newsletters, my studying for school next semester. I feel uninspired, weak, and discouraged. I know I need to snap out of it, but I just can't do it. I'm between two lives, the one I have now and the one I could have had. And I'm mourning that life. I've even been going to church, and I'm not even religious; when I hear the pastor speak about love and affection and family, I start to cry.

I saw a therapist on and off after Jim's first relapse, before we moved to the city. She always told me to give myself a break, not to be so hard on myself. People talk about a defining moment that opens them up to who they're supposed to be and what they're supposed to do; I'm waiting for mine. The problem is that I know, deep down, that I can't just sit around and wait for it. I have to make it happen. In fact, nobody but me can make it happen. But I'm just not at that point.

I need to take life one day at a time. Get through that day and not worry so much about the next. I'll try to focus on what I *can* do right now as opposed to what I *can't*. I must be doing as much as I can, though, because right now I don't feel like I can do any more.

Jim is out at a meeting now. He seems to be on the right path in the last couple of weeks. He's been hanging out with good people, who have a lot of clean time. I can feel it. I know when he's not taking the high road, like people with arthritis know when it's going to rain. But I'm caught in a bad place, and I don't know how to get out of it. I love him, despite everything. He's the father of my child, which is a bond I don't share with anyone else in the world. No other man will love or understand Sage like I do. I'll never be able to say to another man that "our daughter has your eyes" or "I can see your smile in her face."

As an outsider looking in, I would tell myself that this man is selfish, to move on. "Get out of there. Run!" Why can't I do that? I sit alone and cry. I beg for an answer, for courage I can't seem to muster. I'm too ashamed to tell anyone how I feel. I've never wanted to take my own life, but I don't feel strong right now.

If I didn't have this computer and these words I write, I don't know where I would be. When I was in college, I used to walk down a long, winding road in the middle of a beautiful farm. There were vines curled around the thick wooden fence, plush green grass, green trees, yellow flowers, blue skies, and horses grazing in the pasture. I would take the walk alone, always alone. Nature was my calm, my solace. The smell of the dirt, of the horses and the grass, was so alive, so sweet to me. It's the only place I can go in my head that is safe. I picture walking there with Sage, holding her hand and looking into her eyes and smiling at her and letting her know it will all be okay.

I wish I could get there. I wish I could give that peace to her.

Sunday September 27, 2009

I wish I could say things have improved since my last entry. Jim went out Friday night to a meeting and then out for dinner. I found out that he's recently started talking to a girl he dated a long time ago. I confronted him, and he said they were just old friends. I also told him to delete Fred and his brother as Facebook friends if he really wants them out of his life. He did, and then the next day, he friended them right back again. He looked me in the eye and said he had no idea how that could have happened, that he had nothing to do with it. It took me an hour to get him to admit that he did it.

He said he was picking up some NA people and going to a special meeting in the city and that he'd be out late. I took Sage bowling and invited some friends back to the house for wine. We had a great time, and they didn't leave until two in the morning. For the first time in a long time, I wasn't even thinking about Jim. He called while I was cleaning up and said, in a sarcastic tone, "I'm calling to tell you I'm in the city on my way home. I figured you'd be waiting up for me." In a split second, I went from distracted, to anxious, to extremely concerned. My gut told me he was high, just like it told me there was no meeting.

I was asleep for two hours before I woke to the sound of Jim coming through the front door. His eyes were glazed over, and his tongue was so swollen he spoke with a lisp. He was calm. All the signs were there again.

He let me go through his pants pockets, and I immediately found two sticks of Xanax. He said he did take one because he had a panic attack. (*Gee, good thing he was prepared!*)

I called Katie, the girl he went out with, because he gave me his phone and her number was all over it, as was Fred's. All the signs pointed to more than just Xanax. She called back and told me she was not with him romantically. I told her I didn't care. I told her the story he gave me about where he'd been. She said they went out for drinks and to a show with a bunch of people.

That fucking liar.

There was an e-mail to Katie on his phone:

> Yeah, I'm going through a rough divorce. I tried the Leave it to Beaver thing for a while but it didn't work out. I'll be back in the city in the next few months.

I guess his life with me is a joke to him. He tried the family thing, the sober thing, and impregnated me and figured out it didn't work for him.

What a prick.

I checked his voicemails and found a message from a lawyer who was starting eviction proceedings against us because Jim hadn't paid the rent in two months. Jim had told me he *had* paid the rent, without my asking.

This man is sick.

I didn't give him a drug test. What's the point? He refuses to cut Fred, his cocaine supplier, off. He doesn't want to do that to him. He claims there is no need to insult people. He says he has no interest in Katie, that they dated in eighth grade for about a week. In the morning he could see I was at my breaking point and said he wouldn't go out anymore. I said,

"I really don't care. Just go. I don't want to see you right now." I said we had agreed that if this happened again, he would move out. He said he would move out on Wednesday, after he got the bridge loan. I'll believe it when I see it.

I am on a mission. My feelings for Jim are over. He is my enemy now. He is so fucked in the head he can't tell what reality is anymore. He can't tell the truth, and I think sometimes he actually believes his own lies. This is not just an addict I'm dealing with. Our life is in ruins. I actually gave him $100 today—money for food and bills—so he could go to the NA event. Instead, he used it to go out, drink, and get high with a girl. Fred, Katie, drugs ... I don't know how many people are in line in front of Sage and me in Jim's life. *Unbelievable.*

Nothing he can say can hold me here. He has fucked me over and pulled on my heartstrings for the last time! I knew it was over a while back, but I was still not ready. Now I am. I am determined to move on. I cannot waste one more minute of my life on this man. He has strung me along for years, and I have got to get out from under him. I have a long and nasty road ahead of me, but it'll feel good to be in control of my own life again.

I want a separation, and I want it now. I'll go to court if I need to to keep him away from Sage. He's in no shape to be with her, not even for a weekend. Even if he's clean when he picks her up, he could take Xanax while he's with her; she'd be left alone because she couldn't wake him up. No fucking way.

The last thing I said to him after he talked to me with his nasty attitude and abusive tone was that he should take his illegal gun, put it in his mouth, and blow his brains out because that is what I would do if I were him.

I am ready now. Good night!

Monday, September 28, 2009

From: Amanda
Date: Monday, September 28, 2009 11:23 PM
To: Susan
Subject: Life

Yeah, I could use a hug to say the least. I'm at the end of my rope. I just spent another weekend of Jim promising he wasn't going out and then coming home in the early morning high as a kite, and out cold all day, sleeping in front of Sage. He's lying about everything and using what little money we have to go out and buy drugs and drink. It's pathetic. I think I have to move out of this house soon. It's scary: I locked myself in my room with Sage last night.

Thank goodness for my family, though. I don't know what I would do without them. Thank you for the kind words. I need the positivity right now.

Hugs,

Amanda

From: Susan
Date: Tuesday, September 29, 2009 12:03 AM
To: Amanda
Subject: Re: Life

Okay, Amanda … big hug. You need it.

Nothing you write sounds good! You're definitely between a rock and a hard place, and I wish I could offer you salvation.

What's going on?

Is Jim performing at work? Or is financial tension so much that he's escaping? You seem really stressed, flabbergasted, blind-sided. You say you're going to need to move out … is this because Jim is unwilling to leave "his" house, or is it because the both of you can no longer afford your mortgage, the brooklyn development, an apartment for Jim, etc.?

Whatever it is, know that you are not a failure. I know you're disappointed that you're not independent. But you trusted your husband to support you while you built your own life. You're going to pull through. If anyone is a fighter and resourceful and makes things happen, it's you.

Whatever happens, please know that I'll never judge. If you separate, I'll support you. If you stay with him, I'll support you. I'll never look down on Jim, no matter your decision. Life throws crazy curveballs. Friends are needed. I'm here as much as I can be.

Love you,

Susan

Tuesday, September 29, 2009

Yesterday I had Jim call the seller's attorney for our house, in front of me, because of his message that we were being evicted. He called on speaker, and the attorney verified everything I had suspected. He said Jim had broken every contract and agreement they had made, and had also sent them fraudulent wire transfers and bounced checks. The attorney directly asked if Jim was going to have the rent of $8,500 by the end of the day (*$8,500?*

Jim had told me it was $6,000). If not, he would file the eviction papers. He said, "Jim, are we clear? We need $8,500 by the end of the day, or we want you out."

Jim said, "So you're telling me you want me out or you want the money. What are you saying? I need to talk to my attorney if you want me out."

The attorney, clearly astonished by this statement, said, "Are you kidding? Jim, you don't need a lawyer to know you have to pay your rent or you'll be evicted."

Jim said, "Are you telling me I don't need a lawyer? You are actually telling me I don't need representation? That doesn't sound good to me. Are you asking me not to speak to a lawyer? That's it—next time you hear from me, it will be through my attorney."

Jim's answers didn't make any sense; he was answering questions he wasn't asked. I don't know how else to describe it.

After this call, we went to the bank so Jim could prove he had a bridge loan clearing in his account. When we got there, I walked up to the door with him, and he said, "Wait out here. Why are you following me? What are you, a psycho?"

Yeah, there is something wrong with me.

Of course, I went in. I listened to the clerk tell Jim that his account was closed and another one was overdrawn. He kept asking strange questions, trying to get an answer he wanted. She finally said, "Sir, I don't understand what you're trying to say. It's very simple: if you want money in your account, just deposit a check. You do not need to go to your branch manager to deposit a check, sir."

He still tried to convince me that I didn't hear what I had just heard.

"Jim, I know you don't have the money. Let's work on this together. Just be honest with me, and we'll figure something out."

"What are you talking about? I have the money. You heard her say that my account's blocked. I have to talk to a branch manager."

More lies, followed by more lies. This man is not making any sense.

But today I finally took back some control over my life. I don't feel like I want to feel yet, but it's a step in the right direction. I went to our accountant to settle the fact that I haven't filed taxes. It had actually been five years since we filed. I started by back-filing three years separate from Jim. I started to pack and moved a ton of boxes to my mother-in-law's basement to prepare for when I need to leave. She had a lot of space and said I could store my things there. It felt good to get the ball rolling and not be stuck in the same place. It feels good to know there's hope and that I'm at least starting to get out from under this mess. I won't know what's really going on until Jim tells me what's happening with us financially, but I can start to take back control of my own life.

I can keep envisioning myself somewhere else, with someone else, in a life the way I always pictured it. I will never expect perfection, but that's okay. I don't want perfection, and I don't want what Jim has been trying to sell me but couldn't deliver—it's not realistic. I want reality. I want mistakes, but I want to know about them and I want to be a part of them. I want my life, with all of its faults, to be my own.

Chapter 5: Empty Promises—October 2009

From: Amanda
Date: Thursday, October 1, 2009 3:43 PM
To: Katie
Subject: I apologize about calling you …

Katie,

I know you've been friends with Jim for a long time and I'm sure you're a wonderful person. Jim, however, has been having trouble with lying and using drugs for a long time now: pills, cocaine, drinking. I called you because when Jim came home high at 4:30 in the morning he told me to take his phone and call whoever I wanted to prove he was at a Narcotics Anonymous function in the city with his sponsor. Your number was all over his phone, so I called.

I don't appreciate you saying I was being manipulative. I wasn't. I simply asked you if you were with Jim because he told me he was not with you—just like he said he was not out getting high. He came out of a detox program at SI University hospital in July, and started using again soon after. He's been using in front of our five-year-old daughter, so please excuse my behavior. I'm at a point where I don't know what to do anymore. My daughter and I are in the Little Steps program at the YMCA for children with drug-addicted parents. You mentioned that your ex-husband was trying to get sober, so I imagine you can relate to what I'm going through.

I apologize for making you feel uncomfortable. I never meant to, but you may never understand the things you will do for your own child and her safety. I'm just trying to leave this situation with our daughter in one piece. If you think I'm making this up please feel free to call Jim's mother. She remembers you fondly and said she'd be more than happy to speak with you to verify everything. She was also there that day I called you. Her number is xxx-xxxx.

Take Care,

Amanda

From: Katie
Date: Friday, October 2, 2009 5:02 PM
To: Amanda
Subject: Re: I apologize about calling you …

Amanda,

Jim didn't speak badly of you at all. I don't think this e-mail is fair to him or, to be honest, to me. What do you want me to do with this? And how did you even get my e-mail?

As I told you, I don't do drugs and Jim did not do drugs with me last Saturday. He has never done drugs with me in all the 25 years I've known him.

I'm sorry to hear you've been having a hard time. And I do have some understanding of how hard relationships and sometimes their breakups can be. But people need to tell their own stories, Amanda. It may be hard or almost impossible for you to imagine, but maybe your version of Jim isn't the only truth.

You have the right to tell your own story, the way you see it, to your friends when you are ready. But so does Jim. It's a basic human right, to tell your own story in your own time.

For now, the only two times I saw Jim (and once was about business), the feature story he had to tell was about Sage and how great she is and how crazy he is about her.

I do think it's manipulative to try to get information about one person through a third person. I do think calling strangers at 5 a.m. and tracking them down—well, I'm nobody to judge, but I don't think people do that when they're in a good place. I think if you were my partner I'd probably not want to tell you I was going to meet an old friend you didn't know either. But what I think is irrelevant to your situation, your marriage, your child, your life. I never got the chance to know you and now I have only just caught up with Jim in the past couple of weeks. I don't have anything to do with your relationship.

I hope nothing more than that you guys work this out and come through stronger and wiser and with more love and understanding for one another—for both of your sakes and for your daughter, whether you pull that off as a couple or as respectful mutual parents. But until that time I would appreciate not having any further direct communication from you.

From: Amanda
Date: Saturday, October 3 11:11 AM
To: Katie
Subject: Re: Re: I apologize about calling you …

Katie,

I called you out of desperation and fear for my husband's safety. I'm obviously not in a good place, thus the apology.

When you have a daughter and you depend on your husband for her livelihood and he's out driving around all night on alcohol, Xanax, and coke, then you can tell me when it's appropriate to call the "friends" he hangs out with.

If you're naïve enough to think it's okay to drink with an addict and get involved with a man who's still living with his wife and child, then you're morally bankrupt and I can only thank God you never had any children of your own. It sounds like you are interested in Jim. He is the worst curse I could put on anyone. Good luck with that.

Sunday, October 4, 2009

Today was Family Day at Sage's school. All the happy families were running around playing games. I went with Jim, Sage, and my mother-in-law, who spoke not one word to her son. It was awkward, but I felt okay, and that was most important. I think Jim wants to be a good dad—he just has no idea how. I'm continuing to see just how sick and sad this man is. He lies about whom he meets and when, even after I tell him that the lies hurt more than what he is actually doing. He can still look me in the eye and tell me something I know for a fact is not true.

He went out for some things this morning. Before he left, he said again that he was sorry, that I'm not insane, and he hugged me from behind my chair. He said he knows he's sick, but I know he has no idea what he's actually done. I think during the three weeks he just had clean, he started to deal with his emotions and all that he had done and it became too much to handle, so he used again. It's going to take a lot to actually deal with how he has screwed up his life; quite frankly, I don't think he has it in him. He has to start over without me, and with Sage only partly in his life.

I have it in me—it won't be easy, but I can start
over. I can make a new life for Sage and me.

Until I can leave this house, I've told Jim he can go out on weekends and get as high as he wants, but not in a car with my name on it. He'll have to catch a ride, call a cab, or get his BMW back. If he comes home high, I'll call the police. It's the only way I know right now to cope with an awful situation. I got a magnet from my YMCA group with a saying on it: "I did not cause it, I cannot control it, I cannot cure anyone else's problems or addictions, but I can learn to cope."

I've been so caught up in the lies and the drugs and the deception and the pain and anger that I'm taking it all too personally. How can I not? It's happening to me, and it's being done to me by the man I once loved. There has to come a point where I let go, or it will eat me alive. I am coming to that point. Sometimes I slip up, but I know I will get there, and I'll look back on this and thank myself that I had the courage and strength to get out. I'm starting to see the forest for the trees for the first time ever: I'm just now seeing that life doesn't have to be this way.

Tomorrow is a new day. Tomorrow will be better than today.

Tuesday, October 6, 2009

After Jim's father died, his younger half-brother had no money—he'd been living off their father. Jim decided to support him. He paid his rent and gave him money for food; his brother seemed unable to hold down a job. Much like Jim, he lived in a fantasy world. Jim got him into an apartment (owned by my cousin), and his brother would pay his cable bill before he even thought about paying the rent. He had no job, but he had money to buy cigarettes and smoke pot every day. Here we were, a young family just starting out with a baby, and Jim was supporting his younger brother's ridiculous lifestyle. When I found out, he denied everything, telling me I was insane, that I had no idea what I was talking about. My cousin—Jason—came to me because Jim's brother had stopped paying rent. Jim paid it, and when I confronted him about it, he denied that, too. He denies it to this day, despite the fact that Jason had no reason to lie.

He's taken me on vacations and bought me expensive jewelry that I didn't ask for. I've never really been interested in material things. I do enjoy the freedom to go out to dinner or take nice trips, but Jim's always been focused on what car we drive or where we live. I make do with what I have. I'm good at being frugal, yet making our home *look* expensive—a regular Martha Stewart. In our first house, I painted every room myself, redid the kitchen, the floors, the yard—everything I could do myself to save money. I remember being eight months pregnant, wearing a mask, so I could paint the nursery and the attic that he had promised to take care of for months. When we needed yard work to be done, I was the one pulling trees out of the ground at seven months pregnant. I didn't think much of it at the time. I would ask Jim to help, and he'd say, "Pay someone to do that. That's why I work and make money: so I don't have to do those things."

The house was so beautiful that people would ask me who decorated it or chose the colors. That made me happy. Jim was never happy. He was always looking to get the biggest, best TV or some other status symbol. I let it go because I realized we were different—if that was something he wanted and we could afford it, then it was okay. I allowed him to put two car leases in my name that I could never afford on my own because he wanted to have his Mercedes and an Audi SUV. I had excellent credit and he had awful credit, so I agreed.

Sage and I have a daily affirmation we read in the car. I just keep reading it and hope one day I can really feel it and believe it and give myself a pat on the back: "I love myself, and I'm doing the best I can."

I'm learning how to depend on myself again. I'm doing the best I can, and that will only improve over time. I don't want to be alone; I want to find someone I deserve. But it's true that if I don't fix myself first, I'll never be able to be happy with anyone else. I've been avoiding that and covering it up with Jim's illness, but life has come full circle for me now, and it won't allow me to hide anymore.

It's time to get up, pick up the pieces, dust myself off, and worry about Sage and me. What Jim does still bothers me, but I'm bouncing back a lot quicker now. I'm starting to realize that he's the sick one and I don't want to be there with him anymore.

I don't want to be there with him anymore. I don't want to be sick.

Friday, October 9, 2009

The week went by okay for the most part. Jim promised me money again from a settlement he says he was awarded, but I haven't received anything. I have to pay three parking tickets he got in the Audi, but I don't have the money. Every day he's getting calls because his credit cards are maxed out and he can't make the minimum payments. Most of our bills are not getting paid.

Last night I got something in the mail and called Jim about it right away: it was a warrant for his arrest. It said that if he didn't turn himself in, he'd be arrested publicly if caught.

A few years back, a colleague—"Bob"—sued Jim over ownership of the Hope Street building. I don't understand the dispute, but it has something to do with differing views of what commission Bob should get for helping to purchase the building.

Two and a half years ago, I had to go to court because Bob had put a lien on our house—*my* house, which I had bought before we were married. We had to hire lawyers and spend the day in court to prove that the house was mine. My only defense was that the house was purchased before Jim and I were married, and that the house was only in my name. I remember sitting in court, so angry with Bob and thinking what a horrible person he must have been. He was trying to put a $250,000 lien on *my house*. The judge was a kindly older man who clearly felt bad for me in this situation, and I could see he was irate with Jim. (I saw him a few weeks later at a political function, and he half-joked that I really should not be involved with someone like my husband. I should have valued his opinion and heeded his warning, but I let that one go right over my head, which was exactly where I wanted it at the time.)

Ever since that lawsuit, we have been periodically getting served to appear in court. When we were living in the city, servers would run after me if they saw me leave our apartment. Since we moved to this big house on Emerson Hill, we didn't hear a peep until a few months ago. Jim had to surrender his personal property—which wasn't worth much—in order to satisfy the sheriff until the case was settled. He was ordered to bring in his motorcycle, a custom Big Bear Chopper worth $35,000.

There's yet another story underneath this one: Jim owed Jason money, and he took the bike to Jason's house as collateral, which was where it was when the police requested it. Needless to say, Jim couldn't produce it because Jason wouldn't give it back to him (and I can't say I blame him). Jim eventually did pay Jason back, with little interest, but Jason claims that Jim put him in financial hock over this loan. Jason said he found himself making promises he wouldn't ordinarily make in business because he thought the money was coming in a day or two and when he got the money back it was nowhere near what he was promised.

He said Jim once actually took him to a Citibank to verify a wire going into Jason's account; the banker told Jim to leave because nothing like that existed and what he was doing was committing fraud. Jason said Jim had him drive hours away one day to show him a piece of property he wanted to use as collateral. He also gave Jason a post-dated check for $50,000; he told him it was going to bounce but not to worry, that he would have the money wired the next day or get him a cashier's check—neither happened.

Anyway, I have no idea right now why Jim had to go to court and turn himself in to the same judge who threw out this case two years ago. He may have to spend the weekend in jail, which doesn't bother me one bit. I have no money to bail him out. If he wants out, he can call Katie. I am through with this.

I called Jason to warn him because when Jim left, he was yelling that this was probably all my cousin's fault and he wanted to kick the shit out of him. I had said, still trying to be nice about this, "Do you want me to come with you and explain to the judge that we were never served anything? What do I do if you get arrested? Call a lawyer?"

"No," he said. "I'll handle it. Think of it this way: at least you'll know where I am."

"That's not funny. Do you not see that your life is unmanageable?"

And he left. So here I am waiting to see if my husband will be in jail all weekend. Jason asked me today how it is that I am okay, how I wake up each morning and start my day. "I don't know," I said. He said I was one of the strongest people he had ever known. He said he can't understand how I make it through the day living with this man. How I wake up and look at him and all that he's done. He said the biggest fight between him and his girlfriend is over whether the gas bill gets paid on time and who's going to bathe their two daughters. "I don't know, Jason," I said. "I guess I am strong. I must be, because to me this just feels normal."

Tuesday, October 13, 2009

Jim did not get arrested. The warrant was vacated, and he claims he has to go to court in a couple of months to countersue Bob. He went into the city Friday night for a meeting with his sponsor. He knew he couldn't use the Audi, so he got his car back from Meg and took that into the city. I don't know why I bothered, but I asked him to please stay clean because I didn't think I could handle another episode.

I had a bad feeling that tonight was going to be a long one, so I took Sage to my parents' house, and my dad came back to stay with me in case Jim came home high. He didn't want me to call the police, so he called Jim and told him if he was out getting high to not come home because he didn't want to see him get arrested. Jim said he wasn't high and that he'd be home in an hour or so.

My father and I went out to a pharmacy at eleven o'clock to buy a drug test that I had waiting when Jim walked in the door after midnight. He seemed sober and took the test immediately: it came up clean, but it was only for coke—not for Xanax.

The weekend went by uneventfully. We took Sage to soccer practice and to her friend's house for a playdate. Jim went to a midnight meeting Saturday and came home exactly when he was supposed to.

But I still have a sick feeling in my gut, knowing
that I'm not through with this yet.

Monday was Columbus Day, and I went out Sunday night with a couple of friends. When I returned home, Jim was awake, having a panic attack. I asked if he needed anything, and he said he was going to try to sleep. He slept the whole next day, under the influence of a double dose of antianxiety pills and a "natural" sleeping aid prescribed by his doctor. Who really knew anymore? Sage was upset because her daddy wouldn't get up and play with her, which made me upset again—I had to deal with this little girl's feelings being crushed by her sick dad on the couch.

Last night Jim and I watched a movie called "Man on Fire," with Denzel Washington, about a man who would stop at nothing to save a little girl he bonded with and loved as her bodyguard. Jim said he understood that feeling, and that if anyone hurt a hair on our daughter's head, he would stop at nothing to destroy them. I said maybe then he could understand how I felt about him. I joked and said I was a "Mom on Fire." I told him how angry I was with him because of how much he hurt Sage and that I didn't know how to deal with that anger. I said I wanted to just hit him sometimes, to hurt him physically the way he had hurt her.

"Do it," he said. "Seriously. Hit me as hard as you can. As many times as you want."

"What?" I said. "I can't do that. I can't!"

"Yes, you can," he said. "Do it. I want you to."

I stood in front of him and he waited for me to hit him, but I couldn't do it. I knew it would feel good, but I couldn't get up the guts. I started talking about how I could picture him snorting that shit up his nose, and how he refused to stop talking to Fred, and how he lied to me about meeting with Katie, and then I pictured our daughter's face and her disappointment, and I tightened my fist and hit him on his left side. He wasn't even fazed. He said to do it again, so I did. And again, so I did. And I did and I did and I did until I stopped picturing those images in my head. I felt in control for a brief moment, feeling that he was getting a small piece of what he deserved. He said I hadn't hurt him at all, but that he hoped I felt better.

I was flushed with guilt and sadness, and then felt righteous and angry beyond all measure. But then I realized I could hit him a million times and it wouldn't erase the past. It didn't change my situation: the man who was destroying so many lives was still standing in front of me.

How can I hurt him if he isn't afraid of hurting me? He does it with such ease it almost seems effortless. As if I don't matter, and this divorce is easy. He's never tried to win me back or ask forgiveness or even ask if I'm okay. Never, not even once.

Last night I had the best night's sleep I've had in a long time. I dreamed I was at my mother's with Jim, and we were lying on the couch together, cuddling, spooning, and just breathing. Everything was silent, calm, and he had his arms around me and I felt safe again, something I hadn't felt in ages. Then we were outside on my mother's porch. The weather was warm and breezy, the sun was shining, and I was hugging him. Sage was standing nearby playing and looking back at us and smiling. I wish I could go back to that place where I felt safe and warm with my family.

I want to sleep soundly again, and I want to stop
the nightmares. I want to start over.

Thursday, October 15, 2009

Tonight I took Sage to the Y and went to my group. I always sat quietly and listened but never uttered a sound. I spoke for the first time since we started going. I told them today I looked at Jim's cell-phone calls while paying the bill online and saw that he'd been texting Fred and calling Katie every day. When I confronted him, he started yelling that I needed to stop looking through his shit because we're getting a divorce and he doesn't care who I talk to or whether I date. It hurt me. He was still lying to me, now about a woman. I told the group that he lied about everything, in every area of our life. A woman in the group said that was normal, that drug addicts do lie about everything. The counselor said, "How do you know a drug addict is lying? His lips are moving."

I told them about my home drug testing, and they asked me why I do it. I couldn't really answer. Why *am* I testing him? It doesn't really matter anymore, does it? If he's high or not makes no difference to me, because I have to move on with my life with Sage.

I have to create normalcy again within my own life regardless of what state he's in. I am letting go, slowly, but it's hard sometimes. Why is this cycle so addictive to me? He's moving on, finding a girlfriend, and doing horrible things in front of me without a care in the world how I feel. When I go out, he doesn't even ask me where I went or who I was with because he really doesn't care.

Why do I still care about him when he doesn't care about me?

I have vowed that as soon as he's out of my life, I can and will move on. For me, being around Jim every day is like a recovering addict living with a dealer. In the group, they tell me that even when we're together, I have to emotionally detach myself from him. They're right, and I also have to minimize our time together: no more outings with him and Sage and me, no more meals together, and no more TV together. To begin, I've decided to stop speaking to him—not to be spiteful, but to take myself out of his life. Right now, that's the only way I know how to do it.

Remember, Jim is not Jim, and Jim is not my friend. Let go and let God.

Sunday, October 18, 2009

I said I wouldn't speak to him anymore, and when I woke up the next day, I didn't even say good morning. He took the Audi to work, and I didn't hear from him again until Saturday at 11:00 a.m., and then only because his mother called him. He left no word, and I didn't call or text him. When he finally did answer his mother's call, he said that he was okay, that he had no idea why I would be worried—that I didn't want him home anyway, so he was staying out at much as possible. When I asked where he was, he said it was none of my business.

"So you get to disappear, and I'm left with Sage and the responsibility? That's not parenting. You can stay here, so don't tell me I said you can't."

He said he'd stop in to get his stuff and try to be here early enough to play with Sage, but that he had to work, on a Saturday. I don't know why I keep allowing this man to disappoint me, but I am disappointed. He came over for about fifteen minutes, dressed Sage, and left promptly.

His mom went through the exact same thing with his dad, and she told me to stop being disappointed, to expect nothing from him, either financially or emotionally. She said she understood everything I was going through and that trying to make Jim see what he was doing wrong was useless. The drugs and the addict behavior came first for him. She's right about everything, I know, but understanding it doesn't make living it any easier.

I still can't believe this man I married would ever hurt me so much.

Monday, October 19, 2009

Jim came home Sunday morning and told me he'd been going to meetings all weekend with his sponsor and that he'd take a urine test. I came home at 3:00 p.m. and he drank water, but by the time he went to bed, he said he still didn't have to pee. At 6:00 a.m., he brought a cup into my room. His sample was obviously diluted and hardly smelled like urine at all. The test strip confirmed it was probably diluted; there was water dripping down the sides. I shouldn't even be testing him, but a lawyer I consulted with recently, said it would be good to have the results to show to a judge if necessary. I told him I would wait until he peed again.

I went to see Jason yesterday to work on the menu for his new restaurant. He told me stories about Jim and just how unbelievable everything he did was. He told me about fraudulent wire transfers, Jim's strategies for withholding payments, and how he manipulates people. Jason said Jim would write himself a check from one account to another for millions of dollars and then print out a statement showing that there was that much money in the account before the check bounced. Believe it or not, this worked on a number of people. He would send others on wild-goose chases from bank to bank to verify wires that he had "coming in," all bogus.

Jim never had the money to pay people back. He'd ask obscure questions to confuse them. "Sure, Jim," they would say. "Okay, that makes sense"—but they could never verify his claims. He once took Jason to his lawyer's office and asked the secretary questions about the Hope Street building and its closing; she said she couldn't confirm definitely, but from what she had heard, what he was saying could be true. Jason said Jim would flash paperwork in front of him and quickly tell him what it said, rather than let him read it for himself.

Jim once showed me an account statement from Chase, saying he had more than $3 million in it. But there was a minus sign in front of the money, and I said it looked like a negative balance to me. He said that was because the money was on hold. Jason said he had gone to the bank with Jim many times, and that was always his excuse, that his account was frozen or that the money didn't clear or was on hold.

Jim's friend Derrick worked as a manager at our local Citibank, which Jim would try to use to his advantage. Derrick told Jason that Jim often asked him to lie and say money was in his account when it wasn't, or that a wire was coming in, or to bail him out of one story or another. He became so frustrated with what Jim was asking him to do that he wanted nothing to do with him anymore.

Jason told me more about the time Jim "sold" him a house that turned out to be owned by someone else. Jim worked with HUD, a New York agency that bought up foreclosure properties. Jason gave him $14,000; after six months, he was still waiting to get a key. Finally he physically went to the house—Jim told him to go in through the back door because he still didn't have a key himself. The place had been improved: new refrigerator, fresh paint, and so on. Jason called Jim, who said that was normal, that HUD had to bring the place up to code for the buyer. Jason heard someone upstairs and began yelling, thinking it was a squatter. A man came down with a baseball bat and said to get the hell out of his house. Jason explained the situation, and the man showed him paperwork proving that he had bought the house two and a half months earlier.

Jason calmly called Jim and asked to meet him. When they met, Jim smelled like pot and apologized, saying he didn't know what had happened and that of course he would get Jason his money back as soon as possible.

At the time, I heard a different story from Jim, who said he repaid Jason right away; Jason said he got the money back in installments over time. He said one time Jim came to his house and told him and his girlfriend that he'd get them the money and not to worry—just not to tell me because I would divorce him.

Jim said Jason was trying to extort him for money. Jason finally came to me and my entire family to confront him. Jim managed to turn around everything that everyone said. Jason even had a friend there who said that Jim had written him false checks and signed over false property upstate, and he wriggled out of that one, too. Jason said by the time Jim left, he was so confused he could hardly stand up straight.

By the time I left Jason's yesterday, my head was spinning, too, because he was starting to put together all the pieces that had been missing for so long. He began to verify things that had been driving me crazy: things like the phony bank statements and bounced checks, getting bankers on the phone—things that I had never mentioned to anyone.

> *My husband is a con man, a drug addict, and a compulsive*
> *and pathological liar. I've been conned for my entire*
> *marriage. The house we live in is not ours, we own nothing,*
> *and we owe more money than I ever dreamed.*

Jason asked me how I look at him, how I go home every day, and I said,

"Because he has me on the floor with his foot on my neck. I'm trying to get out from under him, but he's strong."

Wednesday, October 21, 2009

Jim agreed to give my father his BMW to sell to get his money back. When I asked him where the car was, he said his friend Meg had it, but that he couldn't get in touch with Meg. Now, Jim talks to Meg every day, multiple times a day. When I suggested he text him, he said Meg didn't have text service, which I know to be a lie. He finally told my dad to get the car from Meg himself. I texted Meg and asked for the car back, and he said that he didn't have any car, that Jim knew what was going on, and that he'd give it back when the building closed. How could he not have it but promise to give it back? Beats me. This just gets crazier by the day.

Meg recently spoke to me about Jim, who he said put him in a financial hole over this building; I'm assuming Jim gave him the car as collateral, but Jim denies this vehemently. He promised my dad the car at the same time he promised it to Meg. Meanwhile I just looked at the title and, he hasn't even paid it off.

Today I spoke with Jim's lawyer about his closing, and once again, much of what I said was news to him. He was very clear about what he knew, and when I talked to Jim, he told me he never told me those things, that I had heard what I had "wanted to hear." Jim told me that the bank was handing over proof of funds, or a bond, to the bank (the seller), that the lawyer was handling this, and that the closing documents were being drawn up. The lawyer knew nothing of this, and again Jim yelled at me, telling me I had no idea what I was talking about. Now I realize what his tactic is when he's backed into a corner: he turns defense into offense to knock me off my guard.

I asked him about the settlement that was due two weeks ago and got another story: now he says he has to come up with a fee to get his money. I need this money to move out and pay my dad back. I called his bluff and said that I was sure my dad would loan him the fee. He backpedaled and said it would be easier for him to do it himself than for us to go to a lawyer and verify everything. *There's nothing to verify Jim. Nothing.*

One good thing is that I am genuinely, for the first time, distancing myself from Jim emotionally. I don't get upset when he yells, and I'm not taking things personally—I know he's not well. What I was feeling on Sunday— hopelessness and despair—is slowly turning into a calm feeling of control over my own life. My hope that things might work out, that Jim might make a recovery and turn his life around for his family, is gone. I am okay with the fact that I am moving on without him. I look at him in a real light now, with no false hopes.

It's still an awful situation, but at least I am getting better.

Sunday, October 25, 2009

I went out Thursday and Friday nights and hardly slept, but I had fun. It felt good to be around healthy people and to do something for myself without a thought of Jim. When I came home late on Friday night, he was home watching Sage, but I had put her to bed before I left. At 3:30 a.m., he had called to see if I was okay, whether I was drunk; he said to leave the car and take a cab if I needed to. I was fine, and when I got home, he had left me some vitamins with a note saying to take them for my hangover. The next morning, he was supposed to get up with Sage and let me sleep, but he didn't. I ended up getting up at 8:00 a.m. and staying with her while he slept all day. I don't think he was high, but I can never be certain.

Last night he went to a birthday party for someone in NA. I woke up at 5:00 a.m. and he hadn't come home, so I texted him. He texted back that he'd be home soon. I knew what I was in for, but for the first time I was okay. I did get a little nervous, but nothing like before. I felt stronger. I didn't feel hurt. I didn't get upset or take it personally. *This is a sick person I am dealing with.*

He walked in and offered to take a drug test. I agreed, and he came up positive for coke. I didn't yell or ask to look at his phone. I just said, "You are so sad." I told him to sleep in our bed so Sage wouldn't have to see him. He denied the drugs as usual and swore on our daughter's life that he was at the party all night and that the test was wrong again.

I laughed and said, "I know you used, you know you used, and you know I know it, so let's stop playing games. I know you were out with Katie. I don't care anymore. I just want you to stop driving the car around high, so I'll take the keys."

"Believe what you want to believe." He put the keys on the coffee table.

"Whatever. Go sleep it off."

His efforts to lie were becoming more and more pathetic.

When I came home later and he was awake, he had nothing to say. I asked him why he kept doing this. I said if he wanted to stop, I would still help him get into a program. He said I have no idea how cocaine makes him feel, that he'll be ready when he feels like it.

I can really see how sick he is, and that it has nothing to do with me. This is a hard realization for a co-addict to come to but I am a co-addict. My mind is clearer for the first time in a long time, and I feel good about it. I'm coping, taking care of myself and my daughter, and I'm not trying to control him anymore. I hit my own bottom, and I'm slowly coming up. He's not okay—far from it— but I am, and that's what matters. His sickness doesn't define me anymore.

I'm stronger than I've been in a long time.

I placed an ad online today to sell my furniture. I have some cash stashed away: not much, but enough to help me move out. I'm waiting to see if Jim's closing is for real. Soon I am out of here. I've learned some valuable lessons from this situation, and the most important one is to never lose myself again in anyone. I've allowed myself to put up with too much.

Tonight I was driving, the air crisp, the sun setting, the trees covered in fall-colored leaves. I smiled. I'm not free of this situation yet, but I was free in my mind. I'm taking the lessons I've learned and leaving my mistakes behind. I smiled, and I thought of myself and what was good about me. I smiled and meant it.

I smiled.

Tuesday, October 27, 2009

Jim finally woke up, and I gave him the car keys for the week. I said he couldn't use it on the weekends, but I'm sure he will. It's silly to argue with this man anymore because there's no controlling an addict, especially an angry one. He broke his phone somehow and was out of it on the couch for over forty-eight hours. He woke up today and showered—for the first time in three days. He told me it wasn't a problem for our daughter because she didn't see him high and he didn't use during the week, that all she sees is him sleeping.

That's exactly right: all she sees is her father sleeping.

Jim yelled at my father the other day, insisting that he was going to see his daughter no matter what. He blew up and hit the refrigerator door when my father said he wasn't going to see her if he was high. (*What was the difference, isn't Jim always high?*) He was always either in a rage or passed out cold. Jim actually told my father that just because he only takes the drugs while he's out—if that's even true—that it's okay, that he's some sort of responsible parent. All sanity has left this man, and only now is mine returning.

I got a call today from the broker for the house we're living in, saying she has to start showing it again. Jim's world is crashing in on him—on us—and his double life is starting to collapse.

I've been looking for jobs and working with Jason to help open his restaurant—maybe I can work there. I'm hopeful, though not living in a fantasy. I know I'm on my own with my child. Before her bath last night, Sage asked me to write the words, "We need help for," on paper, and then she wrote "Daddy."

"Mom," she said, "we need help for Daddy to get better. We need help to get more money, and we need help to find a place to live." No child should ever have to utter those words, to worry or be burdened with those feelings.

I looked her in the eye and said, "Sage, I love you, and I never want you to worry about any of those things. You leave the worrying to me. Mommy will take care of everything. Everything will be great."

"It'll be okay, Mom. I know it'll be okay."

How can a child be this caring and insightful at five years old? I have been blessed with an amazing little girl. I will take care of her. I will make everything right, no matter what I have to do or how I have to do it—with or without the help of her father. I will protect her from his drug abuse and anger if it's the last thing I do. I will not allow him to be in her life while he's like this. Even if this money does come through, he won't be able to bribe me with it.

My silence is not for sale. My daughter is not for sale.

Saturday, October 31, 2009

Grieving is a process. Sometimes when I think I've taken some really big steps forward, I find myself taking a step back. Hopefully it's just a small step and I can continue forward. Today is my five-year wedding anniversary with Jim. He spent the last two days out drinking and drugging, and I spent them trying to remain calm and move on. I went on a date last night to a Nets game because I couldn't bear to be alone and I thought it would take my mind off our anniversary. I had fun, and it did, but I came home alone and slept through until morning.

Sage stayed at my parents', and I woke up alone. I don't know what I expected, but my feelings were still with me. I cried and cried until finally, out of weakness, I texted Jim, "Happy Anniversary." I didn't know where he was, but I did know what he was doing, and even though he had called me a cunt the last time we spoke, two days earlier, I was remembering our wedding and not what we had become.

I had told him we would be gone for the weekend because I didn't want any problems for Sage on Halloween. When I woke up early, I went straight to my parents' house. It wasn't long before he texted me back:

Happy anniversary. It will be another sunny and warm day as in the beginning and now at the end. I thought you were staying out for the weekend, but when I came home I saw you were back so I went to a friend's. My phone is dead so don't be nervous. I will be able to charge it in the car at 9 when we go out to dinner, so call you then if you can't get me over the next hour for any reason.

I texted:

If you could see into my heart you would know everything—but I know you can't right now. All I have is the memory of that beautiful day and the way you looked at me. But the rain is comforting because maybe my tears will blend in with the raindrops and people won't see the pain behind my eyes. I was home alone hoping you might remember that day, too. My heart hurts and every breath I take is a painful reminder that I can't compete with what you've chosen in your life now. I just keep choking on my tears.

I'm gone now, so you can go home. I'm not there, but my heart is and always will be. I'm just a ghost looking in, outside of my own life. All I wanted was to lay my head down on you. But when I think of how you look at me now I know I won't make it through this day, so I'll choose the memories.

He texted:
> I am sorry you are so sad. Although I don't show it I am sad, too. I hope for better days for all of us, and I want nothing but for you and Sage to be happy. When will you be home again?

I texted:
> Sage and I will be happy again one day. We just need space from this, space I hope will come very soon. She's cuddling up next to me right now. She knows I'm sad, and I can't wait for her to see me smile again. I never wanted any of us to be this sad. If someone had told me that I would be alone today, of all days, without you, I wouldn't have believed them. I want to reach out to you, but you're not there. I'm standing alone.

> Five years ago today I wasn't, and no one can take that away from me. No one can tell me that wasn't real, because I can still feel it. I can see your face, and I can see it now in Sage's eyes and smile. Whatever you're going through won't last, but Sage and I will be here to prove there was good in your life.

> Today is a rough day for me, more than I can express. If you're going out again, you won't be home anyway, right? I may stop in to shower tomorrow and will be home tomorrow night. We won't interfere with your plans.

He texted:
> Just wanted to know. You said you were spending the weekend away, so I didn't know when you were coming home. Are you going to be back tonight or tomorrow? I need to make plans out if you're going to be home tonight.

I texted:
> Yes, yes, we won't be home, so you can do what you want.

He didn't respond again.

I went home to pick up some clothes and saw his bottle of Viagra. It used to have four pills in it—now there were only three.

We were married in New Hope, Pennsylvania, in a beautiful bed-and-breakfast on one of the most gorgeous days ever. Jim's sister-in-law caused a huge argument right before I walked down the aisle. Both Jim's niece and nephew were in the wedding party. Her children were running around and Jackie suggested to her she might want to stop them or their clothes would get dirty before the ceremony. She was insulted, and overreacted about Jackie's statement and ran back to Jim's brother. His brother started yelling at me before I entered the chapel. He told me that Jackie and I should shut the fuck up and mind our own business. Jackie meant no harm but they were acting like animals. His mom sided with them and ignored us and cried through the whole wedding. But for some reason, when I walked down that aisle and saw Jim's face, I knew it would be okay. He was always able to make me feel at home and safe.

Five years ago today, we swore we would be together forever, and we pledged this in front of everyone who was important to us, including our four-and-a-half-month-old daughter. Jim has broken every vow we took and has broken my heart along with them. What began on such a promising and hopeful day, filled with love and excitement for a new life, has ended today, with hurt, anger, and betrayal such as I never could have imagined.

I've managed to come out of this, though, with good friends who have been there for me more than I can say. There are people who have been kinder to me than I ever would have expected, offering their homes, their time, their friendship, laughter, and kind words. I'm grateful for this and don't know what I would do without these friends, both old and new.

I'm lying in bed next to Sage at my parents' house, ending what should have been an amazing day, writing these words, shedding these tears, and hoping to catch my breath. I want to breathe easy once more. I want this ache to go away, my heart to stop tightening, *for this to just end!*

My mother said something that sits with me tonight. She said, "What would have happened if you hadn't saved his life? Imagine if you just walked out that door all those years ago. But you did save his life." I think about that a lot. Jim hasn't stopped using for three days. The last few times he did this, he almost died, but someone was there to stop him. Why is he here? Why does someone like this keep on living and destroying when there are good people who want to live, yet who die?

I'm not here to save anyone's life but mine and
Sage's. I'm here to save our lives.

Chapter 6: He's Gone—November 2009

Sunday, November 1, 2009

Jim is still missing. I came home to shower this morning, and I could tell that he didn't sleep here but he had been here. The light was on downstairs, and two chairs were pulled from the basement table as though people had been sitting there. There were cigarette ashes in the bathroom sink and remnants of white powder on the walnut table. I entered Sage's bathroom and froze as I looked down. It looked like someone had washed up in her bathroom. There was bright blue Listerine spit up all over her white sink and mirror and the bottle was spilled over on the counter. I don't know where he is or whether he's even alive, and I don't want to know. I'm scared, and I don't want to deal with what he'll be like after a four-day binge.

My dad is sleeping here tonight, and I'm going to look for a job tomorrow. Our time in this house is limited. If this keeps up, I won't be able to pay basic bills anymore, not that I've gotten much from Jim over the last eight months. He has abandoned us emotionally, and now physically as well.

In a way, it's easier to not deal with the irrational behavior and the anger. There's no one here to call me a bitch or a cunt, no one to yell at me, no one in a haze of drugs, no one to push or threaten me, no one to worry about. He's actually doing us a favor by staying away. I hope he won't come home tonight, but tomorrow is Monday; he'll have to come at some point to shower and dress, even if it's just for a few minutes in the morning. I hope he doesn't do even that. My life with Jim is so full of problems, deception, and ups and downs that I haven't felt peace for years. I don't even remember what it feels like.

But I want to. I want to feel peace again.

Monday, November 2, 2009

I woke up this morning and got Sage ready for school. Jim never came home and never contacted me. I looked for work, handing in applications at hospitals and faxing my résumé to as many places as I could. I went to see how Jason's restaurant is coming along—he does want me to work with him, but he won't be open until January and I need money now. When I was there, I got a text from Jim asking if I was home—nothing more. I didn't bother to respond. I guess in his stupor he forgot that I told him I'd be back Sunday night, and apparently he also forgot that Sage goes to school on Mondays.

On my way home late tonight, I followed a hunch and drove by the Hilton—Jim's car was there. Inside, they told me there were two people checked into the room—they said the other person was male, but who knows? I tried to reach Jim. He didn't answer his cell or the hotel phone, and he didn't answer the door when the clerk knocked for me. I drove home angry.

He's spending hundreds of dollars getting loaded in
a hotel room, and Sage and I have nothing.

Tuesday, November 3, 2009

The addict came home and started a fight with me again. He threatened to call my lawyer and settle things in court, because he will not agree to give me anything.

Screaming, yelling, threats, cursing, fighting: I'm at the end of my rope, and he's just at the beginning of his. He is a monster, a drug-addicted monster, who's keeping me hanging by a thread with the promise of money. He yelled at me in front of Sage, and I remained calm until she left, trying to cushion the blow for her.

He started by saying, in front of her, that I kept him away from her all weekend. He said it was my fault that his heart was broken, and that he couldn't see her because I took her away. I said that was simply not true and that I had told him we were staying away from Friday until Sunday and would be home Sunday afternoon. I saw him Friday morning (Sage did not) and not again until Tuesday afternoon.

"That's bullshit," he said. "I called you. I texted you Saturday but you never answered me, and I texted you Sunday."

"No, you didn't," I said. "The last I heard from you was Saturday morning, and I told you our plans. You said if we came home that you weren't going to, because you didn't want to see me."

"Sage," he said, pointing a finger at me, "Mommy is the reason I didn't see you. Mommy keeps me away from you."

Unbelievable.

"Sage," I said, "that's not true." I turned to Jim. "Please calm down. Stop this."

"Fuck you," he said. "I'm done talking to you. No more drug tests; my lawyer said that's done. You don't tell me what to do. Have your lawyer talk to my lawyer. I'll let a judge decide what you get."

"Come on, Sage, honey," I said, hands trembling, moving to leave the room.

"Mommy," she said, "I believe you. I know Daddy is lying."

"You know Mommy would never do that, don't you, baby? I love you."

"Daddy!" she shouted. "You are *bad*! I know you're doing bad things, like smoking and doing drugs and sleeping all the time. Leave Mommy alone!"

He turned from the basement stairs.

"Yeah, Sage?" he said. "Well, do you know that Mommy smokes, too? And Daddy doesn't do drugs anymore, so Mommy is the reason I don't see you."

I held Sage's hand, took her downstairs to where Jim was sitting on the couch, and said, "Okay, this is enough. I want to say this in front of both of you. Mommy promises not to fight with Daddy. Sage doesn't like this, and it's not fair to her. I will stay calm, and if Daddy fights with me again, I'll walk away."

I knew in my heart that Jim had little desire to see her. He was out getting high all weekend; that's why the drug tests are over. My parents drove over to pick up Sage, and when my dad came in, Jim yelled at him, too, claiming that the drugs aren't the problem, that I am. That it's me that's killing him.

When my dad left, I decided to take the high road. Another plea for peace I never in my wildest dreams thought I would propose. I read Jim my entry from this journal from October 31 to show him that I was not an evil monster trying to keep him from our daughter. I cried while I read it ...

"Jim," I said when I was finished, "I'm not evil. It's the drugs. Where are you?" I tried to look into his eyes, to see something, anything, that I hadn't seen before, any tiny flicker of hope. "Where are you?"

"I'm right here," he said, and he stood up and hugged me.

"I can't argue with you anymore," I said. "I don't want this. I know you're not going to stop using; I can see that now. I know how much pressure you're under and that people are after you for money and that everything's crashing in on you. I understand why you can't stop. I just want honesty. I keep telling you I don't hate you; I'm not mad at you; I'm mad at the disease. I hate the addiction. I hate it."

"I didn't do any drugs this weekend," he said. "Besides, we're getting a divorce, so it's none of your fucking business anyway."

I was not going to bite. "Let's just try and be friends," I said. "I'm not accepting your drug use, but I can't deal with it anymore, either. Let's do what we have to and try to love each other instead of kill each other. I know you can't help it right now, and I hope you get help after you close on the building."

Like waiting for a building to close was a reason to get high!

I knew my words fell on deaf ears. I don't know how I'm going to be able to look at him high all the time, but I'll do it for Sage, for the time being, anyway.

I keep trying to make him see that he's doing the wrong thing, but he doesn't even believe anymore that he has a problem. I know he'll continue to lie to me and he'll continue to fool the people in NA, but that's his cross to bear. I am going against every natural instinct to try and be kind to someone who is abusing me and my daughter. It's only temporary, though—just another month, and then we're free.

> *Please, God, please, Aunt Linda, give me the strength to*
> *get through this and move on with Sage. I need something*
> *bigger than myself to get me out of this situation.*

Sunday, November 8, 2009

A week of more anger and abuse. I don't even know why I'm here anymore. I tried to make peace, and it was okay for a few days. I went out Friday night and met a new guy—he was nice and it was a welcome distraction, but I'm not interested. I don't think I could be interested in anyone right now.

When I got home, Jim was up; he told me he wished he could turn back time and change things. He said that aside from the drugs, he didn't like who he was. He didn't like himself as a person, and he was not happy. A few days clean, and a glimpse of a real person comes back: it's almost haunting, his shift in attitude when the drugs are present. He said I was wrong about the women, that he hadn't been with anyone. He said he didn't want to tell me about the man he was in the hotel room with. But he said I was right about the drugs. This time he said he couldn't stop. He was seeking out the drugs, and he could not stop.

This was scary to hear.

Last night he said he was going to a meeting, but I knew it wasn't true: there's a change in his eyes when he goes out to use. I could see his determination, with empty pockets, asking me for what little money I had made that day from selling our furniture. I knew not to give it to him, but that didn't stop him from trying. He was going to get high no matter what.

I fell asleep early and woke around twelve thirty in the morning. Of course he was gone. I texted him. I know it's probably counterproductive, but I just want him to know I care. Maybe he can come out of this if he knows people still love him.

Embrace the person; deny the addict.

I wrote:

Jim, as you snort that next line up your nose and look around at the sick people doing this with you, remember how Ralph [his child-hood friend who overdosed in front of friends on heroin] died, and remember Sage, how she is sleeping upstairs waiting for her daddy to come home but will one day know what her daddy is out doing. Think about how sick it would be for her to follow in your footsteps. Please put it down and come home to people who love you. Call me, and I can come and get you.

He texted back that he'd be home in an hour, and he called me twenty min-utes later on his way home. I could tell he was high the moment he walked through the door, although he said he only drank. He wobbled and plopped down onto the kitchen chair and opened up an NA workbook. He started to slur and read me the first of the twelve steps. He said he was having trouble with the first step in NA and wanted me to help him with it because I knew him so well. The first step is supposedly the most difficult because you have to accept that you are an addict.

But he kept repeating himself, going over the same question, forgetting he had just read it. It was pathetic. I told him this was pointless because his number-one problem is denial and lying. If he could speak the truth out loud to me, that would be a start, but until then there was no point in doing the steps. He was going to meetings, but then he was going out and getting high.

From the repetitious, looping way he spoke, I could tell he was on coke. He said he was at a diner and met some people who owned a bar; then he said he ran into them outside the bar; then he said he went to a diner; and so on. It was absurd. His nose was running. He said he knew he had a problem, but that he was having a *real problem* thinking he might have to abstain from using anything for the rest of his life. He finally admitted to "dabbling" before his last relapse two and a half years ago, but he felt that he could control it because he didn't need it.

He probably hasn't stopped using for our entire marriage, and I wonder why we've had so many problems. I went to bed. It was pointless to talk anymore.

This morning Sage woke him up so we could have breakfast together. I asked her not to go but she ran down the stairs screaming "Daddy, Daddy, come eat with us." Reluctantly, sitting across from Jim, I was unable to look at him. I felt a hole where he was sitting, and there was an emptiness inside of me. He sat with us quietly, but he was not there with us. All the while, Sage was chatting away about school, or her best friend, but I couldn't hear anything. I couldn't hear her. I could only hear the silence, nothingness. Jim started sniffling, and as I looked over, in what felt like slow motion, I could see thick red blood dripping out of his nose, and running down his face. The blood dripped into his mouth before he seemed to notice. I handed him a tissue and looked away. It broke my heart for Sage to be witnessing this. I was so sad for her and for him.

And what a sad person he was. A person who has no control over his life and who thinks that drugs will help, that drugs are the answer. He was sitting with his family, but his head was somewhere else. The blood running out of his nose was of no concern to him. I could see how he was rotting away on the inside and no longer cared to cover it up on the outside. All he was worried about was taking something more to make himself feel better, to feel whole, to fill the void.

We're sitting right in front of him, but our love
and family aren't enough to fill his void.

Tuesday, November 10, 2009

I woke up to a stark reality this morning. Jim told me he couldn't sleep and had been up all night looking at websites. He was scared about his own health; he said he lacked the ability to feel, to feel for others. He started telling me the truth about lies he has told me over the years.

He said he and a friend once went into a place with call girls, but that he left and didn't do anything. He said he had never cheated on me, but that he had used drugs much more than I knew, more than I even suspected. He was even high on our wedding day, and had snuck drugs onto the plane to our honeymoon because he didn't want to get dope sick. He was taking Vicodin and was on probably four of them when he was walking down the aisle. He has lied to me the whole time we've been married—about our finances, smoking, who his friends are, and where he goes when he's out.

He also said that he lacks feelings of compassion or caring for others. He literally does not feel bad when he does the wrong things. He has no regret or remorse when he harms people. He said the only person he ever felt any love for was me, and that's why he had to marry me. He admitted to doing whatever he could to keep me over the years. He kept everything else separate from me; he knew I was upset about this, but felt no remorse over it. He is only concerned about himself and what he wants and what makes him happy. He loves drugs because they take him away, they give him a rush, they make him feel something.

He said to ask him anything I wanted, because he felt that this urge, this need, to be honest might go away soon. He admitted to doing coke with Fred and his brother in the hotel those four days. He said that girls were there and that they were partying together, but that he didn't do anything with them.

What in the name of God am I dealing with?

He said he had tried to hurt me, to push me away from him recently because he was no good for me, so I could be happy and have a normal life with someone else. He said he was enjoying the cocaine more than ever: in the past, he said, it would make him feel bad, but now it didn't—he was relishing the escape. He said he liked hanging around people "lower" than himself because it made him feel better about who he was. He admitted to going to NA high and fooling everyone. He enjoyed talking to Fred's brother because he was so fucked up; he said he liked giving him advice, even though he never practiced what he preached.

He said he loved Sage, but not in the way he should.

He said he had been up all night researching what might be his issue; he was scared, because he didn't think there was any help for him. He felt like he didn't have any feelings and that this small window of honesty was already closing. He was all over the place, although his words were as cold as ice. His sentence structure was somewhat incoherent, but basically this is what he told me:

He wanted to learn more about his issues. He said he could relate to people's actions, but he was the type of person who lacked the basic instinct to care about people. He acted very well and like a nice guy. People who met him thought he was a nice guy, and even those that knew him long-term always thought he was a loving and caring friend. They knew he had some natural street smarts, which made them respect him, especially if they were not from that kind of life. He said it allowed him to fit in and do things with a street-type person and get along with those who were not from that lifestyle. He said he had been very successful at getting what he wanted, but always the wrong way. He said the more he showed he had no problems, it just made it easier to manipulate others into giving him money to invest because they looked at him as successful. He said it was all falling apart now, and he knew there was truly something wrong with his choices, and although he did feel bad about hurting people, it didn't stop him from doing it. He said he would love to help people, but he didn't understand why it made him feel good to help people that he knew would screw him over. He said he actually felt better hanging around with people like that. And when it got to a point where they actually did screw him, he enjoyed it because he could react

harshly and go after them unmercifully. He said he also had a problem
telling anybody no if they asked him to help them, even if he couldn't
do it. He said he couldn't help leading them on until they would get
hurt even more. He said he had people in his life now for up to ten years
that still acted as if they were his friends because they still believed he
could pull off these deals he was working on. He said those people had
discovered when he let them get close to him that he was not open, not
nice, and lied to them all the time; he was surprised that they still stuck
around. He said they still showed him some respect and put up with him
because they were the type of people that were as morally weak as he was
and thought he was just smart and crazy enough to pull everything off.
He said these people had seen him pull off outrageous shit to keep going
as long as he had. He said he was looked at as someone who would pay
off, and the only reason people stayed around him and helped him was
because they felt he was going to be a multimillionaire. He admitted he
was self-destructive, did everything last-minute, and acted as if things
were taken care of when he hadn't taken care of anything. He said the
sad part was these things were nothing he couldn't actually do or have
someone else jump to do for him. He said he was smart enough to know
he didn't have any true or real friends. He knew he had certain talents,
and that if he put them to good use and put as much effort into doing
things the right way, he could be as good as he pretended to be, and in
the long run, have what he needed. He went on to say he was never sat-
isfied and that he needed instant gratification. He said people thought
he was much smarter than he was because he remembered what smart
people did and said and he was able to act like them. He said he could
fake it, and did it so well that he could be in a room with college grads
and hold a conversation on a topic and sound as if he had a truly unique
point of view, when in reality he was just selling someone else's point of
view and even talking it up better than that person would. He also said
he got really good at subtly controlling topics of conversation that he
could contribute to, and if he was around truly smart people, he would
get to them by saying something to one of them that he knew would

get them to talk about something he was good at. He said he hated to write because it gave away his ignorance. His improper grammar and spelling gave away that not only did he not graduate from college or go to a big-league grad school like most assumed, but he didn't even have his GED. He said he was so busy in high school acting out and making money to impress people that he never went to school. He talked about how he moved in with an older girlfriend at sixteen and missed half of his junior year of high school, and then he got aggravated he could not graduate on time. He said his teachers loved him and blamed his grades on not coming to school. He said all he needed to hear when he went to GED school was that he had the highest score on the entrance exam and was the first they ever put right into a group to take the test immediately, so he didn't bother taking it. He said the reason he was telling me so much about his behavior and capability to do things he should feel bad doing but had no problem doing unless he was caught was that now he was taking bigger and bigger risks. He said he didn't understand why he was like this. He said he was losing control for the first time in his life; he was watching himself do it and didn't know why. He said he did care for a very few people in his life, and those people were all he had to help him feel real, and he knew he hurt them more than anyone. He said he loved his daughter, but got scared when that love for her became numb because he knew she was the main reason he needed to change.

I had to think to close my mouth, to blink even. This was terrifying to hear because it was the truth. There was no denying it anymore. I don't even think the drugs are the biggest problem. He said that he doesn't have even the *basic instinct to care.*

> *I have been lied to, manipulated, deceived, verbally and*
> *mentally abused by the only man I have ever loved.*
> *I blamed his mother, his father, drugs—everything I*
> *could—but not him. What does that make me?*

Thursday, November 12, 2009

Jim is working with the federal government. I'm not privy to the details, but I've known it for some time. I've spoken with the agent, and now realize that this is another life Jim's been leading behind my back. When he first told me, he tried to use it as an excuse for other lies; I bought it at first, but quickly became aware of yet another scam he was playing. When I turned in the drugs I found in Jim's car, the agent I spoke with told me he had given Jim $5,000 for a video surveillance system for our home. Jim had people come and give estimates, but he never had anything installed. Now he was ripping off the government, and for what? Five grand?

Jim decided that he wanted to go away and get help, psychiatric more than anything, but he said he has to discuss it with the agent. They don't want him to go away, and they don't really care about his life—they're just using him to get at bigger fish. I have given this agent contact information for Fred and his brother and told him of their drug use and dealing. I know it means nothing to him, but how can the government turn a blind eye to what they're doing? Both brothers have gotten DUIs in the last six months, and I told the agent they both drive around high every weekend—Jim, too. How is that legal?

Once again Jim has promised not to go out and to give me his keys for the weekend. He says he spoke to his sponsor and will speak to his psychiatrist about his "condition." He also said he'll bring Fred and his brother here and tell them in front of me that he can't see them anymore.

Too little, too late. I've had it. One more drugged-up
weekend, and I'm going to snap.

I told him that if he goes out one more time, if he doesn't have Fred and his brother here on Friday, that I'm leaving with Sage. And I will. It's time.

He told me some more things, maybe small things to some, but devastating to me. He said he did coke while we were at Disney World. He said he had started getting high again right after Sage was born, and that he hadn't stopped smoking cigarettes our whole marriage, that he just kept it from me. He said he got lap dances in a strip club one birthday right before we got married.

He's telling me things that he doesn't have to, and I almost feel like he's doing it to make himself look better. Maybe he's telling the truth. He admitted to looking online for cheating wives just to see if anyone would respond. He said he could have been with Katie if he had wanted to, but that he didn't. He admitted that when he was at the hotel, there were multiple girls in the room, that a couple slept over, and that he and the girls were doing coke all weekend together. The hair stood up all over my body, and I thought I was going to be sick. Could I believe that he was in all of these situations but never cheated? If he was honest about the drugs, then why wouldn't he be honest about this? I guess I'll never know.

Do I really want to know?

I sent an anonymous letter about Fred and his brother and their dealer to the narcotics unit of the police department. I called the hotel they're staying at to let them know what's going on in their rooms. I'm not going to keep quiet anymore. I've been keeping my mouth shut, forgiving and forgetting our entire relationship, but I'm tired of being helpless. I won't do it anymore.

Friday, November 13, 2009

I can't believe the Jim's addiction has taken me to this point. Jim went out again tonight: another NA meeting, another two hours afterward to talk to a friend, and now it's 2:00 a.m. and he's out getting high. He couldn't last two days. After all of Jim's "honesty" yesterday, I found white powder on our basement kitchen counter and a credit card he left nearby. I tasted the powder, and it made my tongue numb. He must have been up all night Wednesday doing coke in our house while Sage and I slept. He told me he didn't sleep; he was up and out early, and acting weird. When I told him about what I found, he said no way, that it might have been someone else's from before, but that it wasn't his.

Did he actually think I was that stupid?

I want to get some sleep, but I can't. I have to think about how I'm going to get out of here tomorrow. This is the last night I ever go through this; I'm at the point of a nervous breakdown but I told Jim I would leave if this happened again. My dad has an apartment he rents out, and he offered it to me but there is a tenant living there right now. The tenant may take one to two months to leave. I can't even think about moving all of our stuff to someone's house temporarily, and then moving it again to my dad's apartment. I have help, I know, but I feel alone. My father keeps talking about God.

If there is a God, how could he let this happen?

Saturday, November 14th, 2009

No word from Jim—not that it matters. I took some more things over to his mother's house. I called my cousin, and she's going to see about free health insurance for Sage and me. I don't have the money to pay $1,000 a month anymore.

I called my friend Jackie, and she reminded me of some things that even I had blocked out. She remembered some things Jim said to me right before we got married, when he was on drugs and I didn't know it; I was distracted by planning for the wedding and taking care of a newborn. He must have been out of dope, because he was angry and spiteful and we got into a fight. He called me a cunt and said I should just leave. He said he could get anyone to do the job I was doing. He could hire a live-in nanny to cook, clean, and take care of our child for a couple hundred dollars a week—what I did for us was replaceable.

I remember at the time feeling more hurt by that than anything he had ever said before. I was holding everything together: being a new mom, dealing with a really bad C-section recovery, and maintaining our household—what he said was so uncalled-for that I was in shock. I told him how much it hurt me, and he said it was just the truth. The next day, he was calmer and apologized.

How and why did I put up with that? Jackie said that at the time, I explained it away by saying that people fight and say hurtful things, and that it was just part of life. She asked how I could marry someone who talked to me like that, and I shut off; I remember figuring that she was single and just couldn't understand the pressure. But she was right. Why did I marry someone who spoke to me like that? Especially when I didn't even know it was probably the drugs talking?

When I look back now, I can see that I loved him and wanted his approval so much that I sold my own soul. I was scared to be alone with a new baby, and I justified everything he said to me. He was also very good at apologizing and acting like he was really sorry he had hurt me. Now I know that he wasn't, that he probably had no regrets.

Sunday, November 15, 2009

Jim is still gone, with no word. Sage is at my mother-in-law's house. I called in an anonymous tip into the police about Fred and his brother. They said there wasn't much they could do without a current address, but that they would look into it. Efforts in vain, even though I know they're futile, sometimes still help me feel in control of my own life. I am so out of control that every little thing I do seems like just a sad attempt to gain control back.

I don't think I will hear from Jim today because I gave him a check for $900 that I couldn't cash; he took it and ran. A refund check came when I cancelled a service we <u>paid</u> for and there were leftover funds. It was in Jim's name so I couldn't cash it. I asked him to please give me some of it but he won't come back until there's no more money, the drugs have run out, and his friends have gone home. At that point, I'll stay away. The less I see of him, the better.

Tuesday, November 17, 2009

Jim finally did come home late Sunday night, and his mother and I were there. I could barely look at him, and I started to cry almost instantly when I saw him. He looked awful as usual, but he had new clothes on. His mother took him outside and spoke with him.

When I talked to her a few minutes later, she told me he admitted he was using drugs to cope with pressure. She and I were upstairs, and I could actually hear him snorting something in the basement. I had never actually seen Jim snort cocaine but just hearing it made me cringe. Horrified, I walked down the stairs and saw him shoving something into the garbage. He retrieved a bloody paper towel to show me he was just blowing his nose. I know what I heard, and I am not going to doubt myself anymore. I know now, that he has no boundaries.

He told me later that he stayed at his friend Nick's hotel in the city for a few nights because he wanted to get off the Xanax again and didn't want anyone to see him. If he was coming off Xanax, then why was his nose so messed up? He admitted to taking Xanax again right after his detox. I can't believe one thing he says, not one. He double-talks and contradicts himself constantly. He was definitely coming off something: he came in jittery, scattered, distracted, and shaking. I have no prior experience with what drug addicts look or act like, but I know when I look at him like this, it scares the hell out of me.

I slept at my parents' house Sunday night only to return Monday to find that he was still there and couldn't go to work because he lost his phone. When I looked outside, I found it lying in the mud, dropped carelessly by the side of his car. I picked it up, and wiped it clean. My first instinct was to go into the house and give it to him, to save him as usual, but something stopped me. I couldn't get into the phone and look at his recent calls like I had done in the past because I didn't know the unlock code, but I wanted him to be held responsible for the hell I was going through and I wanted him to not be able to get in touch with his dealer. He asked me if I saw the phone, and I said no. It was too late to turn back now, so I shut the phone off and put it away.

I was starting to go insane and become diseased, too. This was a turning point for me. I was lying, hiding, sneaking, and doing things that felt awful, thinking maybe it would help Jim somehow. I was trying to keep him away from drugs, which I should have known, was an impossible task. I saw myself living a life dictated by an addict. Every move I made had an ulterior motive. Everything I did, I secretly hoped, would help Jim make a change. I was, and I am, the definition of a co-addict.

I wasn't addicted to drugs but I was addicted to the addict.

Sage and I spent the night at home and I let Jim spend some time with her, but he looked like such a junkie that it was probably a bad idea. Even though I was present, she shouldn't have to see her father looking like that.

The house phone rang, and when I picked it up, it was Fred. I told him not to call this house again, and hung up. Then I thought about what I had really wanted to say. I called back and told him I knew what they were doing together. He admitted to doing coke with Jim, but said it was no big deal. I told him his name was out there and that he had better stay away from Jim, or else. Two minutes later, Jim's half-brother called to say that he was with Fred working at Jim's building, with the demolition crew. *Not only is this guy giving Jim drugs, but now Jim is giving him work?* Jim's employing Fred, an ex-convict, and a drug dealer so he can look legitimate to the police? Fred called back, and both Jim and I answered. Jim said he would handle things. He told Fred not to call the house, and said he'd see him tomorrow and would take care of everything.

This was too much for me. I was deep in a horrible, vicious cycle of lies. In Jim's fit of honesty the other day, he forgot to mention that ten days after detox last summer, he started taking Xanax and hasn't stopped since.

All this time, he was never clean, going to NA meetings high as a kite. No wonder it isn't working for him. He's not ready; he hasn't hit bottom—not even close.

I took Sage to school in the morning, and when I came back, I just let Jim have it. I told him how pathetic he had become. I told him he was living like a lowlife, that he was weak and a horrible father. I said that everything, it seems, is about *him*—everything is on Jim's terms. He's either out getting high with no word to us, or he's home, coming down or unconscious. He's never available to talk to, or to help with our lives, because he's always running away. He lives for himself and his addiction; that white powder is more important to him than me or his little girl. I told him we're home with nothing, not a dollar in my purse. My father has to buy us food while Jim's out spending our money on drugs, booze, and hotels—probably women, too. I told him I'm disgusted with what he's become, that he's no longer human to me. But I told him I was mostly sad because he was the man I chose to be the father of my child, and that's a mistake I'll have to live with for the rest of my life.

I packed up our things. Sage and I were going to Jackie's parents' house— they had an extra room with a bathroom and lots of space (which my parents didn't), and they insisted we come and stay. It was hard for me to accept their help, but it felt better than staying in my own home with a husband who does coke while his wife and daughter sleep. Jim says he's trying to get off the drugs, but I don't care anymore. I know what the weekend will bring, and I don't want to see it. I have to pretend he doesn't exist.

Before I walked out the door, I said: "We're leaving. I don't want to hear from you. I don't want to see you or talk to you. You are sick, and I don't care anymore how you choose to kill yourself. I don't care if you threaten me. I don't need you or your money. Sage and I will get by, but you are not seeing her like this. Never again. When you have thirty days clean, *then* we'll talk about you seeing her again. You said you'd give me $3,000 this week. Let me know if you're going to leave me with nothing, and I'll manage. If not, text me when it's in the house, and I'll pick it up. We'll be gone for a couple weeks, and we'll see what happens. I'm done with your sickness. Have a nice life."

He agreed to everything I said by nodding yes and shrugging his shoulders. He looked almost relieved that he was off the hook and could now have this 7,000-square-foot home to himself. I can only imagine what's going to happen there now that we're gone.

I tried to go back a couple times to pick up some things I forgot, but I didn't go in because his car was there. I went back a third time, and his car was *still* there. It's best if I literally have no contact with him for a while. Don't answer his calls, not that he calls me; don't answer his texts, not that he texts me, either; and don't go there when he's there. This will allow me to start to heal and become uncrazy. I'd like to say "regain my sanity," but that's a long way off.

It hurts that he isn't hurt by us leaving; I can see in his eyes that it doesn't matter to him. It hurts that he never once asked me to stay, or told me he was sorry and meant it or that he knows how much he's hurt me. It's as if our life together never existed and he's writing us off, both me and Sage. It hurts to know that he won't call or text or try and see Sage, that he'll just go on doing what he's doing. It hurts.

It all hurts, but it hurts less being here than being there.

Wednesday, November 18, 2009

I went home this morning, thinking he wouldn't be there because he usually had to be in the city by ten o'clock or so. I was wrong. It's a good thing I didn't just drive off, because he had me locked out of the house. He had bolted the front door from the inside and changed the code to the garage, the only two ways to get in. He said he thought I wasn't coming back so it wouldn't matter. Yes, I said, I was leaving him because he couldn't stay clean, but that didn't mean I couldn't come back when I needed to. The small carload of necessities I brought to Jackie's parent's house wouldn't last a few days. I had a house full of things that I needed to sort out, so I could move out for good. I had my whole life in those rooms.

The more I think about it, the more it makes me angry that Sage and I have to be displaced, that I have to run to different houses to make her lunch or dinner so he can be comfortable. I asked him to find a place so we could come back and stay here until the first of the year. He casually agreed to look, but I knew that was just another line. I could see he was high, way too calm, swaying a little when he walked. Before he left, he asked me when I was leaving, because he didn't want to come back and find me there.

Once I was alone in what used to be our home, I went outside to check the new garage code: it was wrong. He was planning to keep me out. I went upstairs to check on my bottle of Xanax. I had the same prescription for over twelve years and had never taken them. They were gone—thirty two-milligram sticks.

I went downstairs and discovered the remnants of a party from the night before. The basement stunk of cigarettes and booze; there were butts in the garbage, as well as an empty vodka bottle. There was cocaine residue yet again on the kitchen counter, and pajamas and a towel in the downstairs bathroom for a guest. Jim must have stayed in the guest room upstairs because his computer was up there. The bed was a mess. It smelled like cigarettes, and there was a glass with vodka left in it. This all from the man who had told me just the day before that he was coming off everything and trying to get clean.

Thank the Lord I chose to leave.

I took the bolt out of the front door so I could get in later, and I left. Jim called me later from his new $400 cell phone and told me he would have my $3,000 by the end of the week. I am penniless, and I've heard that song and dance before. He also asked where the bolt was and began shouting that I could not go there again unannounced. He said if I want him to leave so we can have the house back, then I need to respect his wishes, or he isn't going anywhere. I will tell you this: if he doesn't give me that money, I will call the police and escort them personally into the crack house that was once our home.

It used to comfort me to hear Jim's voice on the phone, but now it scares me. He sounds like an empty shell, with no emotion. He cares about nothing except whatever will get him his next fix.

I sit here and think about what I'm doing. I'm getting a little stronger, making some strides. I'm lying next to Sage, trying to love her and shield her from pain the best I can. I write these words as a productive release, and then I think about what Jim's doing: drinking and smoking, taking pills, snorting coke, and talking shit—desecrating the sanctity of our home where our child plays and sleeps—and loving every minute of it.

I wake up feeling like I'm living in a movie. But the problem is, I don't feel like it's *my* movie. I feel like an outsider looking in at my own life. I've never seen this side of myself, and sometimes I'm appalled at my own behavior. I look so desperate, angry, hurt, defeated, and physically ill that one more blow could knock me out for good. I see pieces of myself, bits and pieces, and there are not enough to make a whole person. From now on, will I only be bits and pieces?

I want to fast-forward; I want the movie to end—happy or sad, it doesn't matter. What matters is that the credits roll and Sage and I get to walk out of this theater of the insane.

Thursday, November 19, 2009

Today was Sage's parent-teacher conference, and her teacher had nothing but praise for her. She said she was blown away by how Sage thinks, how creatively and outside-the-box she looks at things. She said Sage is doing very well with her reading and socializing, and that she doesn't see any sign of problems at all. She said that Sage is very much a visual learner, and she admires how Sage looks at things. I was so proud and happy and relieved. Sage is doing well. Maybe I *am* doing something right with her. She is an amazing little girl.

My first instinct was to call Jim and let him know of her accomplishment, but he doesn't deserve to be a part of her life right now. I made the decision that he won't be a part of her life while he's using drugs, and I'm going to stick to my guns. Strangely, he called a number of times today, telling me every move he was making. Normally he doesn't call at all, and he ignores his phone when I call him. I answered, was short, and hung right up. He promised, again and again, that money is coming. I just said okay.

Jim owes my dad a lot of money, which my dad would like to use now, to pay off his apartment so Sage and I can live there rent-free—and also, ironically, so he can afford to help us financially. Jim's mom feels so horrible about this that she's offered to pay my dad back herself, out of her 401k. Today she gave him 75 percent of the money. I didn't know what to say. I didn't want to accept it but she insisted, saying she knew that she was helping Sage and me. Jim's malaise has spread like a cancer, through me and Sage to my father, and now to his own mother. I will pay every penny back if it's the last thing I do; I feel sick that she had to do this. He's her son and I understand why she feels responsible, but he's also my husband, and I feel responsible, too.

How can he get away with this? How can this be
happening? I have to believe there will be justice.

Sunday, November 22, 2009

Sage and I are still sleeping at Jackie's parents' house; they have been incredibly generous. Maggie, Jackie's mom, even offered to help out with money if we need it. I felt an overwhelming feeling of love and compassion from her. Friends, family, and even strangers are coming out of the woodwork to help us—I can hardly put into words how touched I am.

I haven't spoken to Jim since Friday, when I went home to do laundry. He looked used up and washed out, like an alternate version of himself. He said he would leave Monday at 3:00 p.m. and that he's doing everything he can to close on the building so he can give Sage and me a life. He said there is a definite closing date now and that I can be there. He also said he'd assign the roof rentals on the building to me that same day with a lawyer. The roof of the building rented a billboard and multiple cell phone towers out. They brought in $15,000 a month. Jim always insisted that he would give that to Sage and me so we would be taken care of.

I asked Jim again just what it was he thought he was doing. I told him he looked awful. I said that everything I was doing, including keeping Sage away, I was doing out of love and to help him. He said he knew that, and to just leave him alone. He seemed relieved when I told him Sage didn't ask about him or want to see him. He didn't seem to care—there was just blankness behind his eyes. I told him again how much I love him and how much he hurt me. I said that if he could get better, back to who he was without the drugs, and if someone could guarantee that he would never do this again, I would want my family back and I would try to forgive all of this.

> *Unfortunately there are no guarantees and*
> *I am not willing to take that risk.*

He smirked. "Yeah, yeah, I know. I've heard all this before. What do you want from me? Just leave me alone."

So I did.

Later I called an associate of his who's also involved with the building. He said there was no closing date yet and that he doubted the lenders would let Jim sign over the roof rent because the income would probably have to go toward building expenses.

> *Well, it was nice for a moment there …*

This weekend was rough for me. The holidays are coming, and as I went out with Sage and my parents, I saw families everywhere doing things together.

I saw dads with their children, and I missed my family. I know I should be over Jim, just disgusted with him, but I miss him sometimes.

I miss being together as a family. Even though he always seemed distracted or removed, there were some good times. There was lots of laughter; he always could make me laugh. There was a comfort with Jim—we'd been together so long that he felt like home. There was love. I don't know now if it was just mine, but there was something there, a feeling when we hugged each other that was warm and exciting and would actually make my heart cave in a little. Jim, the man I thought I knew, was like an old doll. He may have had a lot wrong with him—rips, holes, parts missing—but I loved that doll, no matter how worn-out it was.

Even though I know now that a lot of what Jim told me was untrue, I somehow always felt safe in his arms, felt that he would never let me down, never hurt me intentionally, and that he would always protect me. For some reason, all of those feelings were coming back to me this weekend. Weekends used to be our favorite times together. For the past six months, they've been nothing but horror and fear and abandonment, but this was different. This time, I felt like a piece of me was missing, as if without Jim I would never be the same. Maybe I won't.

Why am I so disappointed and incapable of getting over a man who has wronged me in every way? I have to start looking at why I'm so scared of losing him even though I know I've already lost him. I've been focused on him since I was nineteen. Twelve years. How do I just move on from that in six months, especially while still living with him? This good-bye is harder than I ever could have imagined.

I'm going through the motions of my life, but my heart is torn out and I feel like a zombie most of the time; when I do start to feel, I'm sad, depressed, angry, and hurt. When will these feelings subside? Will they ever? Will I ever be the person I once was before I met Jim?

I was stronger, more self-aware and self-sufficient; I was independent, happy, and positive. People tell me that for a long time now, I've been a very different person: bitter, angry, ready to snap all the time, stressed, uptight, and sad. I've lost myself; I don't even know who I am anymore. I have a sense sometimes, but I don't really feel it. I feel depleted, like I'll never get back up again. I wish I could know when this hurt will end. Will I always carry this pain with me? Could I ever start over with someone else and be happy? Will I ever find someone who will treat Sage as if she were his own?

I want to find someone new and start another family. All I've ever really wanted is to be with someone who adores me and whom I adore and to be around people that I love. That feels so far away. I find myself envious of all the women I see with husbands and children and a beautiful life. I pray they don't take for granted what they have. I never did. Being with Jim always kept me on my toes: I never felt like he really wanted to be with us, so when he was, I appreciated every moment.

I felt so much love and happiness on the occasions when he would give us his everything. I knew it wouldn't last, that he'd start making motions to go downstairs to watch TV, so I relished every moment, excited that he was with us but knowing he'd be done soon. I was always so happy when he would sit with us while we cooked. There were many meals where he would finish eating and just leave the table when Sage and I weren't even halfway done.

I felt lucky that he even wanted to do normal things with us. He made what should have been normal feel special because it wasn't normal for him. Normal was never okay for him. It was never enough, and our time sharing it was always fleeting. I was grasping for something ephemeral because I knew it was the best that I could have with him.

Normal. What I wouldn't give for someone normal.

Tuesday, November 24, 2009

12:30 a.m.

Oh, my God!

I went home today. As I walked in the front door, I was hit in the face by the smell of flower-scented candles and a musty odor. Bottles were everywhere, there were a dozen red roses in a vase wilting on the table, and the fridge was full of leftovers; sauce, meatballs, pasta, desserts, and ice-cream. My pots were on the stove, burned on the bottom as if someone forgot to turn off the gas, and still dirty with food. Wine! Candles! All of the beds looked slept-in—including our daughter's! There were cigarettes everywhere and burn marks all over the edges of the wood end tables and the sofa arms. Some of my clothes were out, including a selection of my underwear lying across the bathroom floor. The tub, in my dream bathroom, was filled with water, and there were wine stains around it; someone had used my makeup and lotion. I was furious.

But what I found next was horrifying.

As I walked down the stairs I noticed a strange smell, something that didn't smell like pot or like cigarettes. Jim had found where I had hidden the alcohol, in a cabinet above the basement refrigerator. Bottles were missing, and when I looked closer, I found a paper bag with a lighter and some glass pipes in it. I just assumed they were pipes to smoke pot. Then I found three opened boxes of baking soda out on the counter. When I looked again at the burn marks on the arms of the sofa, it looked like they were from the shape of the pipes, not cigarettes. There was white residue in the kitchen sink and a metal spoon on the counter. My cheese grater was left out, and had a gray, cakey substance stuck to the inside of it. I suddenly realized that something else was going on other than cocaine and alcohol. I went online to see what crack pipes look like, and the exact pipe I found came up instantly. I looked up how to make crack, and it said with baking soda. My husband was now smoking crack, which explained the odd smell in the house that he may have tried to cover up with candles.

I dropped the bag of pipes and ran out of the house to get some fresh air. I couldn't breathe. Crack. I couldn't fucking breathe. Crack!

I called Jim and told him he had until tonight to get his things before I called the police on him. I was moving back in and he had to leave. My dad came over and stayed with me while Jim came to get his stuff. He was obviously extremely high, staggering around the house as he packed. He could not stand up straight or form a sentence. I am not sure how he drove his car over. He went through the kitchen and took my old prescriptions, all of my vitamins, and any over-the-counter medication he could find, including Robitussin, Claritin, natural sleep aids, and ibuprofen. He took his illegal and unregistered gun and two suitcases. He took the milk and all the food he had bought. He even took a bag of Sage's Halloween candy.

I would have challenged him, but I just wanted him *out*.

He went into the laundry room, presumably to look for the crack pipes, but I had moved them. He took every lighter, the baking soda, and some wooden sticks—which I now realize are used to shove the crack down the pipe—a cup, a spoon, and a candle. He left high, driving with an illegal gun. This was the saddest thing I had ever seen.

My dad doesn't know why I'm so shocked, and I don't know how he is not. I know cocaine is bad, but there's just something so desperate, so sad, about smoking crack. When I think of crack, I think of crack dens, filled with homeless, toothless, low lives, not Jim, not the father of my child. Where can Jim go from here?

He's going to die; I know it. He's going to kill himself.
I can feel it in my bones. He wants to.

4:30 a.m.

I just awoke from a nightmare. I dreamed that my family was here and they all knew about what Jim was doing. The house looked strange: dark, and packed with things, crowded and old and messy. Jason was over, and we were all expecting Jim to come in—we were going to pretend that we didn't know. Jason was standing behind me like a shadow when Jim walked in; for some reason, Jim couldn't see him. Jim looked ragged and had dark circles under his eyes. He was sweaty, and he looked and smelled like he had just come off a long drug binge. I pretended not to know and to believe his story about where he had been.

We went up into the bedroom together, and I played both sides of the field. I was pretending with Jim, but I was actually attracted to his darkness, his evil. I wanted to be a part of it, and I didn't want to let anyone else know. I told him I would be with him. He was acting and talking like an insane person, and he was coming on to me. Jason flashed in front of my eyes, and I could see him lurking in the darkness of the hallway, trying to see what I was going to do. I didn't do anything. I froze between Jason—my conscience—and Jim, the evil. Then I woke up.

I can't sleep. I can feel acid rising in my esophagus, and my heart feels like it's burning. I'm wretched within. I'm twisted. I feel cold and dead inside, like I'm the one smoking the crack. This darkness is consuming me.

It seems like every time I turn a corner and feel like I'm free, Jim is standing on the other side. I can't ignore him and keep walking. I stop and try to help him, but he takes everything I'm carrying and runs away and I have to start my journey all over again, empty-handed.

I have to focus on Sage. She's all I have now. I have no money, no husband, no happiness, and no sanity. I have to keep focusing on her eyes, her smile, her laughter.

I need her now more than ever.

Wednesday, November 25, 2009

Last night I got an earful from people to whom Jim owes money. A friend of his, Juan, told me he's given Jim thousands of dollars over the last few months. Jim told him he needed the money because Sage and I had no food to eat; I never saw any of it. Jim used it to go to hotels, drink, smoke crack, and party. He kept promising Juan money; Juan even did two jobs for him at the building and never got paid. Juan and his brother have given Jim more than $200,000 over the past two years. Jim promised them construction work at the building and said he would pay them back with interest. Nothing yet.

Juan said that three years ago, his friend Patty mortgaged her house to give Jim $200,000 to invest, and she hasn't seen a penny. Patty, who has children, is losing her house, and Jim has ignored her; he had told me this was someone he was trying to "help" with a mortgage. Juan's house is going into foreclosure because after helping Jim, he can't afford his own mortgage. Jim's friend Meg is losing his house because he borrowed $80,000 against it for Jim a year ago. Jim's friend Joel cosigned for $50,000 on Jim's BMW for Jim in exchange for some property upstate that Jim claimed he owned and that Joel was going to develop. Joel found out the property had been sold a year ago; Jim keeps saying he's going to get Joel the money for the car, but in the meantime he's lent it out to a friend, stopped making payments, and now the insurance is up.

Jim used that upstate property six months ago as collateral for someone else, too. He had phony paperwork stating that it was in foreclosure and belonged to him. He's been taking small amounts of money from people, paying them back with interest from other people's money, and then asking for larger sums. After he gets the larger sum, he promises the world: when the building closes, he's really going to take care of them, make them a ton of money. But his scheme is coming to a close. People have been calling me and coming by the house for four days now—evidently he's turned his phone off and stopped returning calls. Everyone wants their money. Everyone wants to know where he is.

So many people's lives are being destroyed to support his lifestyle, and he's done nothing for his family. He's been hurting everyone he touches. He's scammed everyone around him, and it looks like I'm a part of that scam. He's used his family and this big house to foster an image of a loving family man that people can trust. And now he's telling people he can't pay them back because I froze his accounts in the divorce. I haven't even filed for a separation yet! I have no money! He's bounced countless checks. He just bounced one to a lumberyard for Joel's project for more than $50,000. People want to press charges, but no one has yet.

I went to the police yesterday. I wanted to tell them the whole story. No one has even called me back. Everything we have has come from the blood, sweat, and tears of other people. I was keeping Jim safe, but now people know the truth.

Sam, Jim's half-brother, was not part of our life or family for years. I knew Jim still kept in contact with Sam, so I called Sam and told him everything that was going on. We hadn't talked to each other without Jim in the room since we first met. When we spoke we realized Jim talked Sam down to me and then turned around and told Sam I didn't like him and that I said he wasn't welcome in our home. Last Christmas, despite the fact that Sam and I did not get along, I insisted Jim invite Sam to stay with us. I wanted Jim to have his brother around, to have his family with us. Jim didn't get along with his mom or his other brother, and I thought it would be good for him, despite his protests.

Sam told me that when their father died, Jim got the profit from the building he was developing, more than $500,000. He was supposed to split it with Sam. Jim had told me there was no profit in the building and that he actually had to spend money on it. The other owner and investors told Sam that Jim got the money (I never knew this; I just believed Jim) and that he was supposed to split it with him. Jim told him the opposite, and Sam chose to believe his brother because he loved and trusted him.

Where did all that money go?

I thought that Jim's father owed him money that he never paid back, but Sam told me it was the other way around: their father helped Jim start his development company because Jim had bad credit. Jim's father opened a business account in his name and gave him $80,000, which Jim repaid with two bounced checks. I didn't feel bad about this after all his dad had done to his own family, but I wonder now if Jim lied about even that to make me feel bad for him.

That's what Jim did: he made people feel bad for him. He played people against each other. With me, it was his horrible parents, his family, and his childhood. He told me he was molested by his older brother when he was little; now I don't know if that was really true. He told other people that if they told me what was going on, I would divorce him and he would lose his family. Now that we're apart, he tells everyone that I'm the evil one, trying to take him for everything and keep him away from his daughter.

I can't let people think this anymore, so I'm simply telling them. I can no longer let people suffer and have false hope because of his facade. I've told everyone who has called me what's really going on, and they believe me; they can all see through him now. They just needed that little push. He was so believable, so cunning and calculating—he crossed so many lines that people told me they had to believe him because they didn't think anyone would ever go that far or say the things he was saying. That was why I believed him, too. Who would do these things? Who could make this stuff up?

All the people I spoke with said there was always a story, a line, a creation of some peculiar alter-reality that left them with an uneasy feeling. Jim's a con artist, a pathological liar, an addict, and a fraud, and now a lot of people know it. He's on so many drugs that it doesn't matter any longer what's happening around him. He has shut off his phone, his mind, his heart, and his life—now the drugs are taking over.

I've learned that Jim has never been clean in his life. If he wasn't using heavy drugs or hiding pills or smoking pot, he was drinking. He's been an addict since age thirteen. The longest clean time he's had was thirty days in rehab at the age of nineteen.

How can it be that my whole life with this man has been a lie?

Joel asked me how it was possible that I didn't know what was going on. I tried to explain that Jim kept things separate, that he kept me believing because of our lifestyle that things were okay, but the truth was that I loved him and didn't really want to see it. I gave Jim the benefit of the doubt against my better judgment because I thought above everything else that he loved me so much that he would never hurt me. He might have been shady with others, he might have kept things from me so as to not burden me, but he would never leave us or abandon us. I believed that with my whole heart. I knew I wasn't married to a saint, but I thought his conscience and heart lived and breathed with his family, with Sage and me. I thought that, no matter what, he would never break that promise. Now that it is actually happening, I keep finding myself in a state of shock and disbelief, followed by hurt and anger.

Monday, November 30, 2009

I finally went to family court today. I filed an order for full custody, for child support, and for a temporary order of protection. I filled out the paperwork and sat in a room filled with angry and damaged people. I felt disassociated. The fluorescent lights were cold and glaring, and I felt like I was looking down at myself doing something I never imagined possible. Finally, after hours, they called my name, and I walked into the office of the magistrate. She was matter-of-fact and spoke in a monotone, but she could see I was genuine. She looked through me instead of at me. She ruffled some papers, checked some dates, took off her reading glasses, and looked up at me again. She had to decide about the order of protection and child support. I started to choke up as I explained my situation. She looked like she had seen this a thousand times, but she was still sympathetic. She rushed the order of protection and called in a court-appointed lawyer to help me for free. It was done. It felt good. All the threats Jim has made mean nothing, because he never followed through with his promises.

The next step is to get him served. My dad could do it—or anyone, really, but not me. But we couldn't find him. I got a text from him while I was waiting for paperwork. I had texted him earlier, letting him know that the district attorney had called the house and that he needed to get his things because we both had to be out of there in January. He kept asking about the DA, but I didn't respond. I asked him about the money, and he said he wanted to see me alone around 6:00 p.m. I can't pass this up because it could be the perfect opportunity to serve him. I agreed to see him at his mom's, and he said okay. I'm going there and my dad will come later to serve him, but I wonder if he'll even show. I can only try to protect myself. I can no longer be afraid of what he will or will not give me. I sent him this e-mail a couple days ago:

From: Amanda
Date: Saturday, November 28, 2009 7:02 PM
To: Jim
Subject: Sage

Sage left you a message from my phone. She said she wants you to get help and she would like you to be a daddy again.

She is an amazing little girl, and you are missing out on her life. I'm not, though, and other people are there for her who love her. I know you think that's good enough, but no one can replace her daddy. And right now her daddy is smoking crack and everyone knows it.

SAGE SAGE SAGE SAGE SAGE SAGE SAGE SAGE SAGE SAGE SAGE SAGE.

How can you hurt such a wonderful little person, your own daughter? Look at this picture of her. You are a father—or have you forgotten that? How can you spend money on hotel rooms and crack and leave your daughter high and dry? You are already gone. You are not Jim anymore, not a father, not even a person. You are a crack addict. Look at Fred, and whatever woman you have with you and ask yourself if they really even care about you or are just around you for what you can get them. How can you abandon us for them, for drugs, for crack? Every time you pick up that pipe and light it up, there's a little more of your soul taken away. There is no help for anyone who abandons his child.

I live and breathe for that little girl, and you disgrace her.

I went tonight to Jim's mom's house and waited for over an hour. I texted and called Jim, but his phone was off. No one knows where he is, or at least no one's telling. He's driving around with no insurance, with an illegal gun and probably drugs. He's in a hotel or some crack house, and he doesn't want to be found, which means that even if his closing on the building is real, he may not make it and I definitely won't be able to serve him. All my efforts will prove worthless, but maybe it's for the best. Maybe he'll just disappear, never to be heard from again. Never again …

Chapter 7: Just Breathe— December 2009

Tuesday, December 1, 2009

I went to the sheriff's office today because they serve people at no cost, and I still needed to serve Jim. He never showed up at his mom's house, and he's not answering my texts, calls, or e-mails. He doesn't want to be found, and I know why: the way he's acting these days, he can't look me in the eye. He's making me out to be a monster, telling people I kicked him out because we're getting a divorce, that I cheated on him and am keeping him away from Sage and that I want all his money. All these years, I never knew what was going on inside the head of the man lying next to me.

The sheriff recognized Jim's name immediately. He said looking for him would be a waste of time. He had tried to find him in the past for other warrants; they were given a lot of addresses but could never find him. The sheriff refused to take this case. I had to give the file to the court-appointed lawyer, and he had his process server try to find Jim at the building he's buying in Brooklyn. I haven't heard anything yet. If they don't serve him by 9:00 a.m., then I have to begin the process all over again and go back to court myself in two days.

I went on a date Sunday night with a lawyer from Long Island, forty years old and widowed, with seven-year-old twins. I wasn't attracted to him, but being around him was refreshing. He was a real person. He was caring, generous, and sweet and a good father. I wouldn't even know what to do with someone like that. I hope to be healthy enough one day to pick somebody like him—I know I deserve it. I thought Jim was that person, but I was wrong.

Saturday, December 5, 2009

Last week I met with Richard, a good friend of Jim's whom I trust, and you wouldn't believe the things I learned (actually, at this point, you just might). Richard's been involved with the Hope Street project since Day 1, helping to set up Jim's loan and even giving him money. He knows what is going on because Jim's mom called Carl, another good man and a holdover from the days of Jim's dad, and told him everything. Carl was concerned and told Richard that Jim was on crack, needed help, and might never make it to the closing. He asked Richard for his help. I told Richard about Jim's phony heart problem, his drug addiction, everything. Richard told me Jim was always claiming he had heart trouble. He would use this as an excuse of why he was out of touch for a while or need to go to the doctor. I told Richard, Jim's heart was fine, in fact it was very strong. Richard, in turn, told me the following lies Jim had told him:

- He claims we've been living as a family in my father's basement for the last year.
- He says he drives Sage to school every morning.
- He's needed money these past months for food for us. (I haven't seen any of this money.)
- I froze his corporate accounts, and that's why his checks keep bouncing (there was no money in these accounts).
- I'm keeping him from seeing his daughter because of the divorce.
- He has never used drugs.
- He couldn't make it to meetings because of everything going on with the divorce (these were the times he couldn't make it off the couch because he was so drugged up).

- He's a really good dad, a good guy, and all he wants is money to support his family (he's using the money for drugs and hotels).
- He stays home every weekend to be with his daughter and tries to do the
  right thing, but I won't stop arguing with him, so he has to get away.
- People owe him more than $1 million.
- Last but not least, he tried to sell Richard the same property upstate
  he said he owned.

There were smaller lies, but the bigger picture was that Jim wasn't just a junkie lying to get drug money. He's a liar, and his lying is pathological. He's been telling these lies for years, while we've been living in a 7,000-square-foot mansion on top of a hill. Richard told me Jim had held up the closing on the Hope Street building numerous times. He bounced checks to both the title company and the mortgage company. He's behind on taxes and keeps sending corrupt files that no one can open. He sends Carl on wild goose chases, making him drive all over the place to meet him with certified checks to cover the bad checks, at which point Jim will show up with another company check that everyone knows will bounce.

Jim's been bouncing checks to an important lumber supplier, who now wants to press charges, which could further jeopardize the closing. Everyone's trying to contain him because he's like a loaded weapon. He's had a different story for every single person he's dealt with. He knows people's weak points. Whether they're business contacts or family, he knows just what to say to get their money. In the past few months, he's taken probably $10,000 from people in dribs and drabs. At least ten people have told me they gave him hundreds of dollars a week because he cried poverty. All of that money has been supporting his drug habit and lifestyle. I have receipts for hotel stays for $300 a night, with room service and other charges.

Wednesday, December 9, 2009

I tried calling Jim Tuesday and he would not answer my calls, and I got to thinking. I had learned of a website where you can make a phone call that looks like it's coming from a number other than your own—any number, presumably. I wanted to see if he was really down and out or if he was simply screening his calls. I punched Fred's number into the website and had "it" call Jim's number just to see if he would answer. He picked up immediately and I disconnected. Then I called Fred's number with Jim's number showing up on caller ID. Fred answered immediately, too, asking what the good news was, and if Jim got that guy he just left them to meet, to give him some money. The website has options for voice filtering, and I had chosen a phony male voice for the call. When Fred heard it, he started flipping out and asking why I had his friend's phone. He told me he was going to find me and kick the shit out of me. He told me the exact intersection of where he was at that moment. He screamed that I had better get the fuck there now with his friend's phone or else. I agreed and hung up the phone. I was shaking.

This was my chance. I started the car and drove to where Fred was. I was chain smoking the entire way. I did not know exactly what I was doing but I was filled with anger. I knew I was angry at Jim and at his drug supplier. I had a chance to do *something*, and I was going to take it. When I got a block away from them, I recognized Fred's profile in the car; there were two others with him. I drove to the nearest pay phone so my phone couldn't be traced and dialed 911. I told the operator I saw what looked like a drug deal going on. I hung up the phone and drove back to the location. Within minutes, three police cars had the car pinned. I watched from a distance as they patted down all three men, spread-eagle on the squad cars. They searched the car.

I was shaking, screaming and shouting inside. I was afraid if they found out it was me who called the police, they would kill me, but I couldn't pass up the opportunity. Within fifteen minutes, Fred and his friends were hand-cuffed and driven off in the back of the police car.

It was some of the greatest satisfaction I have ever felt. I shouted out loud on my ride home. It felt good to take back some control over my life and do the world a favor, no matter how small or temporary, and get a drug dealer off the street. It felt so good to take away Jim's drug dealer.

Thursday, December 10th, 2009

There was an article in the paper today: Fred and his friends had been found with illegal knives and loose prescription medication in the car and were being held in custody. When Jim couldn't get in touch with them on Tuesday after the arrest, he had nowhere to go, so he went to Richard, who arranged for him to go to a rehab on Saturday. Jim agreed.

Saturday, December 12th, 2009

The night before he was to go, Friday, my father was served papers for Jim at his house and was livid. Jim had been bouncing checks and had used my parents' address as one of his business addresses. I called Jim, and he said he'd handle it next week, but that right now he was going to sleep. It was 5:30 p.m. Fred and his friend had been let out that day on their own recognizance. I knew we wouldn't see or hear from Jim for a long time. He never showed up this morning, even though Richard had pulled so many strings for him. He didn't even answer Richard's call.

I took Sage to a breakfast with Santa. I saw all the proud daddies with their children, laughing and playing. Sage didn't have that. She never had a dad who loved her enough to be there for her. She has a dad who chooses lowlife friends and crack cocaine over his own child.

After breakfast, I dropped Sage off at my parents' house and went home and packed up our stuff by myself. I think I cried straight through until Sunday morning, when I picked Sage up. I had a deep, burning pain in my chest as I boxed up the last twelve years of my life.

*I cried for what I had to live with, for what Jim was, for what he
had done, and most of all for Sage, who had him for a father.*

Monday came and went, and no one heard from him. I was on the phone with Richard when I got served with an eviction notice and a summons to go to court. I was being sued for $550,000 because Jim had failed to pay for the house that we "bought." I knew nothing about the details of our purchase because I had never seen the contract. Now I had it in front of me, and I saw that my name was signed—and I didn't sign it. He had forged my signature! He had crossed out his own name and put mine in its place. Now I was being held responsible for the money he owed.

He had signed a confession of judgment for $600,000 when he defaulted on coming through with the rest of the down payment money. The house purchase price was $1.8 million, of which I had transferred $50,000 to Jim from the sale of my old house as a deposit. He never came through with the rest, but he did send them a fraudulent wire for $200,000 and wrote them a bad check for $700,000. To this day, he says he gave them the money and that they have $600,000 in escrow. He swears the seller's attorney has $600,000 sitting in his escrow account. Well, that's obviously a lie. All he ever gave them was my $50,000 according to the court papers.

I have a court date next week. I've decided to show up without an attorney and just tell the truth. I already talked to the plaintiffs' lawyer and told him I have nothing. If they will give me a hold-harmless letter, I will leave and not prolong the eviction for the nine months it could take for them to get me out with a child. I will also help them prosecute Jim. I hope I can recoup some of the deposit money because the contract was forged and therefore should be void.

How much more can he do to me? Every time I make peace,
however briefly, something else he's done pops up to hurt
me. It's like playing Whac-A-Mole with the devil.

This afternoon there was a knock on my door as I was talking to Richard on the phone. I was home alone with Sage. A stocky, tough-looking guy with a hard face and a leather jacket asked for Jim. He said he was supposed to meet him but that he never showed up. He said he was at our house a couple of weeks ago to go over the Hope Street project. He was bidding a construction job on the Hope Street building and had met Jim for lunch on Friday; afterward Jim had called him up and asked him for money. He gave him $500. (So that was where Jim got his drug money this past weekend.) He said Jim was supposed to meet him Monday and never showed up. He had had people working for weeks to bid this job, and Jim had embarrassed him.

Richard heard everything and spoke to the guy from my cell phone; he calmed him down and took care of everything. This guy was furious. He said it wasn't so much about the money as it was the principle. Jim had taken advantage of him: he wasted his time, borrowed money from him, and then disappeared. I asked why he would give money to someone who was almost a total stranger, and he said Jim told him I was taking him for everything in the divorce and he was coming up short.

So let's backtrack for a minute. Jim knows this guy knows where we live because he's had him over here before. He borrows money from this guy, a street guy. He sets me up as the wife who has all his money. Jim avoids his phone calls and stands him up. He must know this guy's going to show up at our house angry, and that I'll be there alone with Sage. This guy is no white-collar business guy. If I weren't on the phone with Richard, I don't know what I would have done—or what he would have done.

Tuesday, December 15, 2009

Sage has been sick for almost a week. We have no insurance, my cousin found out we are not eligible at this point, but I had to take her to the emergency room. I have to get her some form of Medicaid tomorrow. I texted Jim that she was running a fever, and he didn't respond until yesterday morning, when I got a call saying he was sorry he had missed my text. He said he was clean and he wanted to see her. I told him to show me the detox papers, to call Fred and his brother and tell them he wouldn't see them again, and to take a drug test. He jumped on it. He said he didn't have the papers with him, but that he didn't talk to Fred anymore after his arrest and that he'd love to take a drug test because he was clean as a whistle. I told him to meet me first so I could see whether he was clean.

We met in the afternoon at a Starbucks. I wasn't sure he would show, but then I saw his car pull into the lot. I was shaking. One look at him sent chills down my spine. He walked toward me, and I could see he wasn't there to be nice. He asked what I wanted. He was loud and arrogant. He said the closing was almost compromised because I couldn't keep my mouth shut. He said he could have had money for us right now, but that I had ruined it by telling everyone all the dirty details. He seemed disgusted with me, horrified even.

"Jim," I said, "this is all you. All of it. And you know it."

He sneered and got up. He walked out into the parking lot, and I followed him. I wasn't going to let him off this easy after the way he had spoken to me in there, publicly. "Do you realize," I said, "that you haven't seen your daughter in six weeks? That's a month and a half of her life, Jim."

Then he sat in his car, and I could see that I had hit my mark: there were tears in his eyes. "Please, just let me see her," he said. He was clean, he said, and he just wanted to hold her.

"Fine," I said. "Show me the detox papers."

Well, of course he had them—he just didn't have them *on* him.

"Fine, then," I said. "Call Fred and prove you're not with him anymore." He said Fred's phone was tapped and that he hasn't talked to him in over two weeks and doesn't want to. I'll believe that when I see it.

Then he said, "You have a test? I'll take it right now. You'll see I'm clean."

If he was willing to do that, I had to give him the chance. *Even after everything that he has done, was it my place to keep him away from Sage?* I wanted to do the right thing, but I wasn't sure what the right thing was. I didn't want Sage to feel abandoned. When we got to the house, I told him to wait in the basement; we could both hear Sage upstairs, and I didn't want her to see him. Not yet. I told her to stay upstairs and I gave him the cup. He peed into it in front of me; he knew I wouldn't accept it any other way. We waited, and he looked so confident that I began to wonder if maybe he really was clean. Then, a few minutes later, the test came up positive for cocaine.

"Jim," I said.

"Give it a minute," he said. "There's no way—I've been clean for ten days!"

"Jim," I said again, "why did you even bother?"

"I swear I've been clean," he said. "Look at me! Just let me see her—just a few minutes."

I shook my head. "We had a deal."

"It's because I'm losing weight," he said. "The fat's still flushing out of my body, and it's probably coming out in my urine. Come on, Amanda!"

I heard Sage open the door at the top of the stairs. "Outside," I said to him. "I'm not going to talk about this now." I almost had to push him out the door, but he went.

I looked up at Sage, who was holding the door open. "Mommy," she said. "Who's there?"

"Nobody," I said. "Stay upstairs, sweetheart."

Outside, Jim had gotten into his car. There was both anger and pleading in his eyes, like he didn't know which way to go. He would know soon enough.

"I didn't want it to go this way," I said. "I wanted you in Sage's life; that's why you're here now. But I did what I had to do." I handed him his mail, an envelope with court papers that I had mailed to his last known address, our address, the order of protection.

He took one look at it and there was no more pleading in his eyes, only anger. "What the fuck is this?" he said. "You got an order of protection against me? Do you know what this means? I'm her father!"

"I know exactly what it means," I said. "And so do you." I began to tremble, but I was determined to keep my cool.

"You fucking bitch!" he said. "I never hit you, and I never did anything inappropriate in front of Sage!"

"You liar!" I was beginning to lose it.

"Just let me see her," he said, visibly trying to calm himself because he knew I had him.

"Get out of here," I said, "you fucking junkie."

This man is toxic!

My life is a mess. This legal stuff is exhausting, and I don't know what to do. I'm getting evicted, and I have to go to court because the sellers (our landlords) won't grant me a release of financial responsibility from the house. I know I'm in the right, but I'm scared. I'm overwhelmed, just physically and emotionally beaten, spent. I'm dealing with the repercussions of Jim's actions on top of trying to stay strong and be a good mom, but I'm not doing it well. My patience is running out, and it's hard for me to keep in good spirits for Sage, especially around this holiday.

I don't know where Jim is living or what his plans are.

How can I get him out of my life?

Monday, December 21, 2009

Jim called a few times this past week to let me know what's going on with him. He says he's basically homeless. He says he knows what he did was fucked up, but that he wants to move on. He says the past is the past and he's doing the best he can (blah, blah, blah). He admitted to smoking crack, but says it's not that bad and that he only smoked it to help him come off the Xanax. He was making no sense. (Okay, so you're coming off Xanax—great—but now you're high on fucking crack!) But he didn't sound high anymore.

He begged me to let him see Sage. I didn't want to be spiteful; I wanted to do what was best for her. I asked her if she wanted to see her daddy, and she said yes. She said she missed him and really wanted to see him.

I thought long and hard about this. I would never let her see him alone or high, but I've spoken to a number of people about it. Most, aside from my controlling mother, agree that it's probably best to let her see him, as long as he's clean; the psychological scars of abandonment would be more detrimental in the long run. Better that she know her dad is sick and trying to get better than to think he's just gone. I agreed. I loathe him for what he's done, but I want to do what's best for Sage.

Last Thursday night my mother-in-law agreed Jim could come over while we were visiting. It took a lot for me to be in the same room with him, but I did it for my little girl. She was happy, and I think it was good for her to see him looking and acting okay.

Friday morning I went to the court house for the eviction and the judgment on the house. I went alone, not knowing what to expect. I was nervous. I walked into a packed room full of lawyers in dark clothes, and they looked aggravated, worn, and unhealthy. Most looked like they hadn't seen the sun in years, and were living off caffeine and nicotine. I stuck out like a sore thumb. After a few minutes, the judge walked in. The clerk read off names and cases, and lawyers popped up to say things in legal language I didn't understand; it made me more nervous. Finally they called me to the stand. The lawyer for the owners of the house was there. I explained to the judge about the forgery and said I just wanted to get out. The judge could see I was genuine and honest. He recommended to the lawyer that he get a handwriting analysis and agreed to release me and to pursue my husband if I would vacate the house in an expedient manner. The lawyer looked perturbed. He said he would need to speak with his clients. We agreed to have a phone call, with a court representative, the following week to talk it over and resolve the matter out of court.

I walked out of the courtroom, and the lawyer spoke with me. I showed him my signature. It didn't match up with any of the signatures on the contracts. In fact, the signatures that were there didn't even match up with each other. I said I just wanted to leave quietly and that he could go after my husband. He said he thought that could be arranged but repeated that he needed to speak to his clients. I felt victorious for a moment, but didn't realize this moment would be short-lived.

On the way home, I spoke with my mother, and she berated me for letting Jim see Sage.

"This man deserted you, and we are supporting you now, and you let her see him? How dare you!"

"Mom," I said, "I'm doing what's best for Sage. I'm trying not to be spiteful."

"You don't listen! He did this to you, and then you side with him and disrespect me? You don't know what you're doing! You're just as sick as he is. You think you're so smart, but you have nothing—no job, no career. Look what he did to you!"

"Mom, you can't control me just because you're helping me. I appreciate it, but I'm an adult and I'm doing what I think is best. I may have been wrong, but I trusted Jim. He's my husband, and I never thought he would do this to me. You're supposed to support me, not make me feel bad."

"You think you know everything."

A few hours later, the lawyer called. His tone had changed. He asked why I needed a release if I had nothing. He threatened me with legal terms I didn't understand. He said he was going ahead with the eviction and was going to slap me with a judgment on the house. He said he wasn't convinced about my signature and that he would *never* give me a release. He was trying to intimidate me because I didn't have a lawyer, hoping I would just crack.

I said, "I need a release. If you think I have something, then go ahead and waste your clients' time and money in court, because you can't get blood from a stone. My daughter is on Medicaid. I have $1,500 in the bank. You want that? Go for it. I'll talk to you on the phone with the judge next week."

This is going to be a battle after all. I'm going to have to hire a lawyer to prove I didn't sign the contract so they can't put a lien against me. I'll see what the judge says next week. I'll tell him that now, because of this situation, I'll need more time to move because it will affect my credit. I won't be able to rent an apartment because now I have to scrape money together for a lawyer.

Saturday I took Sage by my mother-in-law's house to see her and Jim. There was a snowstorm coming and she's going to let him stay there for a while, maybe until the closing. I guess if he's there, at least he won't be getting into much trouble; maybe he'll even make it to the closing (if there is one). He finally told me he'd been staying in Brooklyn with friends from NA who had a spare bedroom. We didn't stay long, and at first Sage didn't want to be with Jim. She wanted me to stay by her side, and I did.

When we got home, I needed to put oil in our tank for heat and hot water—Jim had said to put it on his account. When I asked the oil company to do that, they said absolutely not, because he had bounced two checks in a row on them this year. My dad had to give me cash to pay them. When I asked Jim why he would bounce two checks in a row, he said he had had the money coming in, but people didn't come through for him—his stock answer. He was in denial of his own addictive behavior, but I guess that's part of what addiction is.

Sage and I will be moving in a little over two weeks. We'll have a fresh start away from this hell. If I can get a release, we'll be free from this house.

I got a job! Out of five hundred applicants, I got hired at the a Holistic Health School, where I went to school! It isn't much money—only $30k a year—but it's a start. I'll be doing something I love, with great people. They have a gourmet chef who prepares an organic breakfast, lunch, and snack as part of the package. I'll have an unlimited metrocard for commuting, a 401k, health insurance, and two weeks off my first year plus all major holidays and a raise after six months. It's a start at a new life and independence from Jim and my parents. I feel better than I have in a long, long time.

I am no longer sleeping with the enemy—and I have no doubts now about who the enemy is. I harbor no delusions that Jim is someone he's not. It's clear to me now that he's no better than the average drug addict on the street. I'm slowly coming to terms with my reality—not what I wanted or what I think it should have been, but what it *is*—and sorting out my financial mess. At least I know what my financial mess is now! I still have my daughter, and I now have a job. I'm far better off than I was just a few months ago. It still hurts and sometimes my depression is unbearable, but I'm getting through. (Which means, I guess, that it *is* bearable, because I have borne it.) If I can survive this, I can survive anything. Small things that used to bother me seem like a joke now. I look at life differently now. I appreciate everything I have. Things that used to seem major are minor, and what's important is very clear. I have my health, my daughter, food, clothes, shelter, and good friends and family. I'll get through this. I am bending, but I won't break. I'll come out a better person on the other side.

I'm not afraid of much anymore because I've lost everything,
and when you lose everything, there's nothing left to fear.

Friday, December 25, 2009

There's been a change in me between Thanksgiving and Christmas. I'm not saying I'm not sad or depressed, but it's lifted. On Thanksgiving, I was literally in pain and on the verge of tears every minute. Last night and today, I could function. I wasn't happy or excited; I didn't have much feeling at all. There was less pain. I'm emotionally detaching from Jim and getting used to my life without him. Although it upsets me sometimes, it's really sinking in. I'm a single mom—a single, *working* mom—and that's okay. I know I'll find someone else and be happy someday. I won't allow myself to sulk in Jim's misery anymore. I've wasted too much time already.

Jim's mom asked if I would check Jim's phone records for her, to make sure while he's in her house that he's not contacting Fred or his brother. I have his passcode, and I looked. He's still in regular contact with both of them. There aren't many phone calls, but there are tons of text messages. I told his mother, and she was upset.

He's a master at his art, but I can see right through him now. Like in a poker match, I know all of his tells, and exactly how he reacts when he's backed into a corner. In fact, he's so easy to read now that it's almost laughable. If I weren't directly involved, it would be pretty funny watching him try to get out of the holes he digs. It really helps me to see him now in this light—I've always taken it so personally.

My prediction is grim, but it comes from twelve years of experience with him: He'll fool his mom for a while and stay clean. If the building closes, he'll appear to be doing the right thing at first. He won't go to rehab, and he'll start using here and there. Eventually, he'll become a full-blown addict again, but this time it'll be much quicker because he'll have money and be so full of himself. I know this because I can see how clean his conscience is already. Most people who clean themselves up have a hard time with what they've done to others, but Jim is already over that. He just wants to forget and move on. He'll never be truly sorry to me or Sage, and he'll go on manipulating and lying as it suits him. I don't want to be involved in that anymore. The only person I can change is me. The only reaction I can control is my own. I want normalcy and real love now more than ever. I have never and can never get that from Jim, and finally accepting this makes it easier to move on.

I'm different now. I've changed. It's not about what he's doing;
it's about what I know I want—and I don't want this.

Sunday, December 27, 2009

My Aunt Rachel said that Jim's mom would ultimately side with him, no matter what happened or what he did. I insisted she wouldn't, and today I was proven wrong. After she asked me to look at his phone records, I found out without question that he was lying to us both.

This morning Jim called to ask if he could take Sage out with his mom. I told him what I had learned and said I didn't think it was a good idea. I talked to his mom on the phone, and she said I was wrong about this and had ruined the day. She yelled at me and then hung up the phone. I was shocked. She had never been this angry with me. I couldn't get a word in on the phone, so I wrote her this letter and dropped it off at her house.

Dear Abigail,

I'm truly sorry for whatever pain I may have caused you today. Sage is the most important thing in the world to me, and I would do anything to protect her well-being. I trust you implicitly with her, but I can't trust Jim. I believe he's manipulating you and pulling on your heartstrings, just like he does to me. And it sounds like he's maligning me to you the way he did you to me.

You told me to not just believe him, but to look at the facts. The fact here is that he's lying to us about Fred and his brother. We keep allowing him to break his promises, and then we support him anyway. That's enabling. He has to be held accountable for his actions and his lies.

I don't want to stop him from seeing Sage, but I need to be there. I know he's your child and you've done and continue to do everything you can for him. As a mother, I understand that. I hope you understand that I'm only doing the same for my child. I have to do what I think is best.

Jim's biggest problem is that he lies and we all just let it go or give up. You told me that if he contacts Fred or his brother or lies to you, then he can't live in your house; I've said if he acts that way, then he can't be in Sage's life. I've said it a hundred times, and he's lied anyway, every time. What are we saying to him?

Please don't say I ruined the day. Jim's lies and empty promises did. Before, you had distance and could see things. Now I have that perspective and can see things you don't see. If you need someone to blame, of course he'll blame me. You said I'm not giving him a chance. But we've been through hell because of Jim, and we're the only ones bending. He's still lying and talking to drug dealers. In counseling, they tell us not to make empty threats. If the addict doesn't follow through, we have to stick to our guns. Actions speak louder than words.

I respect you and everything you've done. You're a strong and amazing person. Please have a little faith that I know Jim well. You can stay angry with me and hang up on me, and I'll still respect you and know you're a good person. But I'm a good person, too, and I'm trying to do the right thing. I love Sage, and all I want is to move on and be happy. I won't deal with Jim's empty promises anymore. What he says is great—he's placating you now because he has nothing—but what he does *speaks volumes.* I can't keep getting sucked into his lies. I'm sorry. Please call me anytime and see Sage anytime. We love you.

Love,
Amanda

A few minutes after I dropped off the note, she called me. We pretty much went in circles and agreed that we have different opinions. She still insisted I had ruined the day, because Sage was safe with her. I agreed, but I told her that as a mother, I have to go with my gut. I can't keep allowing Jim to see her if he keeps lying and manipulating. She agreed, but said it would have done no harm. I kept telling her that I respect her and I know Sage is safe with her, but that it wasn't about that. She started yelling and said she was going to change the garage code because she was afraid I might come to the house while she was gone and he was there. I told her I would never come to the house while he was there, that she had my word. She said she was going to change it anyway. "Forget it," I said. "Let me know a good time to pick up my boxes." I hung up the phone.

Now I have to rearrange everything. I can put all of my furniture in my grandmother's garage. I have to sell the rest because I have no place for most of it, and could use the money. I will have an estate sale and sell everything I can. I may have to get a storage unit for the rest. She may feel insulted, but what does she expect?

*I don't need him, and I don't need her. I just
need to move on, and keep on moving.*

Tuesday, December 29th, 2009

The call with the court mediator and the seller's attorney was not exactly a win for me. I promised to leave by January 2nd, and they promised to go after Jim, not me, but they refused to give me a release letter. All that means is that I am taking a risk by leaving without one. They can come back and sue me any time, but I have the distinct feeling they know I have nothing and there will be nothing to gain for them.

Whatever happens will happen, I can't control everything anymore. I will take my chances because either way, I have to leave, but more importantly, I *want* to leave.

Chapter 8: Moving On—January, 2010

Saturday, January 2, 2010

"You're going to feel this way until the day you don't."

I love that line, from a song called "Cryin' Ain't Dyin'." It stuck with me over the years, and last night it really meant something. I've been under so much stress and in so much pain for so long that sometimes it feels like there's no end in sight. I had little faith I would ever come out of the fog I was in. I have a staph infection from a hospital stay years ago, and when I'm under stress, it makes my eye and the surrounding tissue swell up, which is happening now. I look like a mess. I've been achy and tired and under the weather for weeks; I feel like my immune system is breaking down. I spent New Year's Day cleaning my dad's apartment and moving some things in for Sage and me, the tenant finally moved out and we are moving in on January 5th. I'm having an estate sale today.

In the next few days, I'll be juggling taking Sage to school, moving, unpacking, and getting everything settled here at the house I am leaving and at the apartment by myself. Then my new job starts a week later. Jim's resting comfortably at his mom's house while I'm running around trying to pack up twelve years of our life together in just a few short weeks. Last week Sage and I had to spend the night in the house with no heat because the oil tank was empty. I had no idea how to check the fuel gauge. The tank ran out in the middle of the night while we were sleeping. I woke up at three in the morning and saw my own breath before I realized it was freezing. I ran to the thermostat and saw the temperature in my room was thirty-eight degrees. I grabbed every cover I could find and bundled us up. I left as soon as the light awakened me. Meanwhile, Jim was sleeping in a warm bed without a care in the world. He hasn't lent a hand or given us a dime for over four months.

But it's starting to feel okay. I'm adjusting to life as a single parent and thinking about things on my own terms. For the first time in twelve years, what Jim does doesn't matter. He's actually not affecting me. I've said, time and time again, even in this journal, that I know what I should do, that I need to just move on. I have here and there, but I've been paralyzed by emotions. I'm not so much paralyzed anymore. I have prospects, a life ahead of me that looks great without Jim in it. I feel, for the first time—and I mean I really *feel* it this time—that I'll be better than okay without him.

Susan came over last night to help with today's estate sale. She's going through a divorce, and we've talked a lot about Jim and her soon-to-be-ex-husband. We've grieved together and gone over our situations together hundreds of times. This time we barely touched on the subject of Jim. We laughed so hard it made my stomach hurt and I had tears running down my face. I haven't laughed like that in over a year. It felt incredible. Something that simple brought me back to life. After we stopped laughing, I felt like it was really going to be okay. If I can feel like that again—liberated, limitless, and uninhibited—for even a few minutes, then there's hope for me. That kind of joy, which had a distant familiarity to it, is something money can't buy. I really was a prisoner with Jim. I was suffocating for years and didn't realize it; the only thing holding me together was my will to succeed for my daughter. But I'm okay now. I feel alive again.

I know there will be setbacks, but I feel that my life is my own. A while back, Jim told me to just move on. He said he didn't care what I did or who I did it with, and he told me to mind my own business about his life. So I did. I slept with someone else. I thought it would help me move on and get to a place I wanted to be. At first, afterward, it felt strange. Jim was my first, and I had only been with one person other than him when we broke up. So this felt wrong, but at the same time, I knew there was no going back, and that felt good. Jim had done so many unforgivable things while we were married that I didn't know why I felt guilty about this. We were getting a divorce and my husband was getting high with women in hotel rooms and hanging out with ex-girlfriends. I thought it was time for me to move on, too. But I wasn't ready yet. I didn't feel any freedom at all. But now that I've had time, distance, and positive people around me, it seems to have happened all on its own, without me even noticing. I didn't have to fool or distract myself into believing anything.

"You're going to feel this way until the day you don't."
I think my day is coming.

I've been talking to a lot of Jim's friends over the last few months, and they've been very supportive and expressed relief to learn that at least their minds weren't playing tricks on them when it came to his behavior. I think everyone can see that I'm genuinely trying to do the right thing. Most important, they know I have nothing to do with his scams and lies.

I've spoken with Richard more than usual lately. He said to me the other day that by telling everyone the truth, I have cut Jim off. I stood up to him and his false threats that kept me scared all these years, and I exposed him. I ended his money supply. I ended the illusion of his boyish charm and his good reputation as a loving father and devoted husband. I confirmed the suspicions everyone had but could never quite put a finger on. He's been lying for so long I don't think he knows the lies from the truth, which is why people believe him: he sounds convincing because he has convinced himself.

If he had to face all the things he really has done, he would have
to admit he's a monster. He would have to see: he is a monster.

I find myself smiling when Richard and I talk and feeling happy after I hang up the phone. I've caught some subtle hints that he might like me, but it's such an awkward situation that I don't know how it would ever work. It's just nice to be attracted to a good person, someone who's real and who, when I hang up the phone, doesn't give me knots in my stomach. I don't know if I'm just looking for a transitional person to help ease the pain or if I genuinely have feelings. I do know that he's the first thing I think of instead of Jim when I wake up these days, so I must need the distraction. I don't want overanalyze it, but it's frustrating to not know whether he feels the same way. I just know it's a good sign that I'm able to think about someone else, because it shows I'm ready to move on.

I am ready to move on.

Sunday, January 3, 2010

It's not only a new year, but a new decade as well. The next ten years have to be better than the last.

Meg's wife Michelle came over today to pick up some furniture. We got to talking, and she told more things I didn't really want to hear but needed to. It turns out Jim did go to a strip club with Meg, and it was Jim's idea; it wasn't for his birthday, and it was after we were married. He "ran into" a couple of strippers he knew there, and they ate together. I'm assuming he was with Naudia, a pill-popping stripper and call girl he's known for years. If he was with her and lying about it, I can only assume it wasn't the first or last time and that he probably cheated on me. I want to know more than anything, but then again, I don't.

Marsha told me about Jim's broken promises to her and Meg. They lost their cars, they're barely able to buy food, and their house is in foreclosure because of the money they lent him. Because he never fully paid them back, she had to pay all her bills with her credit cards, which ruined her credit and put them over $60,000 in debt.

I had asked Jim many times if Meg worked for him, if we were paying him, and he said absolutely not, that they were associates and friends, but that no money passed between them. Turns out that was a lie, too: he had paid Meg to drive around with him every day for nearly a year and a half.

Marsha said she thought I hated her all these years because of things Jim would say about me. After a while, though, she began to wonder: if I was so evil, why would he stay with me? We didn't see them very often, but Meg had evidently invited us over a lot. Jim would say we couldn't go because of me. I told her I thought she didn't like me, either: when I would suggest that we ask them over so our girls could play together, Jim would always say he did invite them, but that they always had an excuse.

We did go to a party for their daughter's birthday a few years ago, and she told me that, beforehand, Jim had told them I might have cancer. She said when we walked into the party he took her aside and asked her not to bring it up because it would make me uncomfortable. Can you imagine? Here I was at this party, chatting away with people and having fun; meanwhile, they thought I might be dying. It's crazy.

One time Meg and Michelle actually did come over to our house. She said she saw early on that Jim was very distant with Sage. She said she never saw him interact with her, that she was always with me or my father. Marsha asked if I had noticed that every time she came near me, Jim was right there, nervous and uncomfortable. He kept an eye on us all the time because he was afraid she would talk.

He made me feel crazy for years, but my instincts were right all along.

Monday, January 4, 2010

I called Jim today, and as usual, he yelled at me and said this has all been my fault. But I was okay. I wasn't upset or intimidated. I told him I was going to go to family court and would try to get him supervised visits with Sage until he gets help and stays clean. I remained calm and rational, and he actually agreed. I saw him later that evening to give him an hour with Sage, I was fine—I just saw a sad, sick individual who happened to invade my life.

Later that day, I found out, through one of Jim's old friends, that he had disappeared from his mom's house over New Year's, just as I had predicted. No doubt he was with Fred and his brother. His mom, who I had thought was on my side, or at least the side of her granddaughter, didn't tell me he was missing, and she lied when I called and asked for him. I assume she was protecting him and didn't want me to think he was backsliding; she said she didn't tell me because she didn't have all the facts yet. He claimed he was in Brooklyn with a friend from NA, at a sober party. I asked where the party was, and he said it was none of my business—a stock answer when he's backed into a corner. I told him and his mom that until he can prove he's clean, he'll have to wait to see Sage. I had just told Jim I would to go to court to see if I could help him with supervised visits, but after finding out he is still using at his mother's house, there is no way. He said he'll go to court, which he has yet to do, so I'm not too worried.

I left our house today to go see the painters at my dad's apartment. The house is almost empty, desolate and barren. I closed the door behind me, leaving behind all that could have been, all that should have been. I was sad, but full of promise at the same time. I can have what I want, just not with whom I once wanted it.

I know what I want now.

Thursday, January 7, 2009

During our first dinner at my dad's apartment, Sage put her little fork down.

"Mommy, I miss our old family."

"What do you mean, sweetheart?"

"I miss when we used to sit on the roof at the old house."

"You mean when we lived on Howard Avenue, when Daddy wasn't so sick?"

"Yeah. I wish it could be like that. If Daddy wasn't sick, then why did he take the drugs to make him sick?"

"Daddy's always had a problem, honey. He can't help it; that's what makes him sick. But you know, we have this new apartment and we're doing great."

"You're right," she smiled up at me.

"We'll have a house again someday and maybe a new family, an even better one."

"Okay, Mommy."

For the last three days I've been moving, packing, unpacking, cleaning, and trying to make everything perfect for Sage. We've moved a lot—four times since she was born. When she was two, we moved from Howard Avenue to Manhattan; at three, we moved from Manhattan back to Howard Avenue; at four, we moved from Howard to the big house on Dune Hill Road; and now, at five and a half, to my dad's apartment. Every time we moved, I took her to my parents' place so she wouldn't have to see me dismantle her room. When she arrived at her new home, her whole room had been completely transported. She adjusts well, and I'm grateful for that.

I know she'll adjust again, but I'm sad, not about Jim so much as about being a single mom without having a man, a dad, around. I miss that. I miss the company and the help, and I miss being a family. But I realize I never really had it with Jim in the first place. What I had was an illusion of that; I guess thinking I had it is what I miss the most.

Next time it will be real.

I'm exhausted. I literally haven't slept in a week. I had the estate sale, had a million errands to run to set up the move, and then had to lug about fifty boxes in ten trips from the house to the apartment. My dad helped a lot, but I did most of it myself. Jim came to the house to pick up his stuff—I wanted it out before I handed the keys back. I had to let him borrow the Audi and help him with furniture, and he helped me with nothing. I even joked that I had a lot to do and if he was looking for work, maybe he could help me move. He shrugged and said, "If you're so broke, how could you afford to hire me?"

He always was one of the laziest people I've ever known. I don't know how I ever fell for him. The good parts were all talk and no action. And I mean *no* action. When I look back, he was sexually dysfunctional for the majority of our relationship. He either had no desire or was unable to perform. I thought it was my fault. Maybe I wasn't as sexy as the strippers he dated in the past.

I haven't been with that many guys, but Jim was the only one who had any problem getting aroused. Those times were most likely when he was on pills, which I realize now was most of the time. They made his testosterone levels drop so much that even when he wasn't on them, his sperm count was below the average for an eighty-year-old man. The few periods when our sex life was good were when he was taking testosterone and abstaining from drugs. The last year we were together, we were trying to get pregnant. We even went to a fertility specialist; I went on medication and underwent artificial insemination twice, to no avail. The doctor tested me and said I was normal, even above average when it came to ovulation, so we had Jim tested. His sperm count was ridiculously low: 400,000 out of the 20 million that was average for a man his age.

Now I look back and realized I have never been so lucky.

I spoke with Richard today. His daughter's been really sick, and I was glad to hear she's doing better. The way he talks about her warms my heart. We spoke briefly about Jim and how the building may actually close in a couple months. An associate of his thinks of Jim as their "golden boy," which Richard said disgusted him. He said that a man who abandons his daughter is not a man, that a man who deserts his family to get high is worth nothing. I appreciated his support. In fact, I just like talking to him.

Saturday, January 9, 2010

Tonight I went out with a friend and had a great time. I didn't even think about Jim. I felt like myself again. I could have fun and not worry about what he was up to. It's amazing to think that our twelve-year relationship could end so viciously and that I could then feel so normal after such a short period of time. In one sense, I can't imagine a life without Jim, but now that I'm living it, I can't remember what it was like to be with him. I can't remember what it was like to wake up to him each morning or for him to come home to me every night. This last year has been so awful that it's become a blur. Any good or "normal" times we had were so long ago and so few and far between that they seem like a dream. I can't remember what it was like to kiss his lips, hold him, feel safe in his arms, or sleep with him. All I see now is a drug addict who lies and abuses with no remorse. Maybe it's for the best that I can't remember; maybe it's a defense mechanism that is allowing me to move on to a new life.

I'm moving on to a better life than the one before.

I start work tomorrow. It'll be a big change, getting Sage and myself ready and leaving early to drop her off at school in time for me to catch the bus. But I'm not worried about that as much as I am about being away from her so much. Her dad's already mostly gone, and now I won't be around and my father will be taking care of her. He's great and he's done so much for us that I'll never be able to repay him, but he's very passive. He loves Sage so much he'll do anything she says, whatever she wants.

He'll never say no to her, and with what's going on, that's not a good thing. He spoiled her as a baby, which was a limited influence, but now it will be far greater. If he has to say "no," he'll say, "Mommy said no." He hates to disappoint her, so he shifts blame onto other people. If she wants cookies for breakfast, he'll say that her uncle ate them and there are none left. Does he realize he's shifting the blame so he always looks like the good guy and everyone else looks bad?

My mother's a different story. She's strong, responsible, and good at finding fun things for Sage to do. I appreciate that, but now that I need some help, boy, does she let me hear about it. She thinks she's entitled to control me because of the position I'm in. The other day I said that ideally I'd like to move with Sage into the city eventually, to be closer to my job. She took it as an insult, saying I wasn't grateful for her help and that I was trying to run away and abandon her. Every time I'm feeling positive, she tells me I won't make it unless I marry a wealthy man. She says I got myself into this position in the first place, that I was naïve and stupid. It feels like she loves that control, saying, "I told you so," and kicking me when I'm down.

I'm grateful for her help, but I don't know why she has to attach strings— that's not love, that's control. I can't take her anger, her yelling and screaming, and her verbal cruelty. She may have a point, but when she acts like that, I just want to run away. I ran to Jim, and now that she sees I'm not a total mess, that I may be able to pull off my independence for real this time, it scares her. She asked my father, if I move to the city, then where does that leave her?

She may be right. Maybe I am running away. The relationship we had while I was growing up was bad. She can't change the past, but she can change how she acts now; yet she doesn't. My father and I barely had a relationship at all, but I don't hold that against him: I look at him for who he is and how he treats me now. Our relationship may not be perfect and I may not always be the most expressive daughter, but he understands what I'm going through and how hard it is and he supports me. He tries his best, and that's all I can ask for. It's all I can handle right now. If I have to deal with my mother's fighting me all the time on top of everything else, I will break. So I have to accept her for who she is and know she will never change and not let it upset me anymore.

For the past three nights, Jim has been calling at seven o'clock on the dot to talk to Sage, as I had suggested he do. I hate to repeat myself, but if I were him, I would be dying not seeing her. He didn't see her for six weeks, and then only three times for an hour or so. Now it's been another two weeks. In two months, he's seen her for a total of maybe six hours. I still have so many questions that have been unanswered, just ignored and swept under the rug. I could write him a note, but what good would it do? I've written plenty already. A friend suggested that I go ahead and write to him, but that I don't send it, that I do it for me. I guess that's what I need to do, so I did:

Jim:

Why haven't you written me? Why haven't you even tried, over the last six months, to get your family back? I know I was a good wife, and Sage is a wonderful little girl. Why, even now, don't you try at all? Don't get me wrong: I don't want you back. But I don't understand how you can just end things so calmly. You never buckle; you never call and say you loved me and you fucked up and you're hurting. The few times I've heard anything of the sort was when I called and begged you to explain why you did this. Why don't you feel worse about our divorce? I've felt so awful I couldn't see straight, and you just went out and got high. I don't understand. I loved you more than anything, and you chose drugs over me. I begged you to get clean. I said we could work anything out. You said all the right things at first, but you did nothing to save our marriage, our family.

Don't you miss me? Don't you miss Sage? Don't you feel anything after we spent the last twelve years of our lives together? What was I to you? Could you really have loved me when you lied and kept everything so separate? You had a whole life that you hid from me when all I wanted was to know all of you because I loved you and would accept anything. What must you think of me? Was I that disposable?

You told me all the time that I was the only one you've ever loved, that you don't know what you would do without me. Was that just bullshit?

You moved on so quickly—new friends, partying, drugs, new

girls—and you threw Sage and me to the curb. After detox I told you I wanted a divorce because I couldn't live like this anymore, and you didn't even resist—not once; not for one minute.

On Saturdays I can't bring myself to make pancakes because it was something we did together every weekend with Sage. You're just fine, but I still can't make a fucking batch of pancakes because of you.

I guess I'm no longer sure there ever was an "us." You kept me caged away from the rest of your life, from who you really are. You are a deviate and a drug addict, and it's just time you admit that's what you really want. Admit that the idea of Sage and me was nice, that you loved us in your sick way, but that getting high with strippers and whores is actually what makes you feel at home. You never, ever showed that side of yourself to me. You've been doing drugs behind my back since we met and everyone but me knew it. Why would you be with someone like me when you know how I feel about drugs? By you staying with me and lying, you made me feel crazy; our whole relationship was like torture. Why would you do that, even to yourself? Why didn't you just stay with one of your other girlfriends who would accept you as a junkie? You would have had a much easier life, and so would I.

Let's face it: it's not about partying once in a while. What does that even mean? You like to go to clubs and do coke so you can feel like a king, even though you know it's just the drugs, and not you. You were getting high every day, taking pills to not get "dope-sick" for years—how is that someone who just likes to party once in a while? That life must be what you really wanted, but you couldn't admit you preferred it over me.

I just want some closure so I can get out from in front of the traffic coming at me as I lie here in the street. You didn't ruin me, but you ruined a big chunk of my life, and I deserve better. I'd like some answers, some real answers. You took twelve years from me that I will never get back. I want honesty from you. I don't think that's too much to ask.

It felt really good to get that out, but I don't think I'll ever get the answers. *Good night.*

Thursday, January 14, 2010

From: Amanda
Date: Thursday, January 14, 2010 9:19 PM
To: Susan
Subject: Thank you

Thanks for letting me bitch. I know I never used to be this negative. Although I hate the commute and the idea of my time not being my own, it does get my mind off my problems, and it's a safe haven for now. Someone cooks for me at work and it's constantly busy, so the time goes by fast. At least I'm finally making some money again. And I'm hoping in time I'll get to change positions and do something I like and make more. We'll see. I miss being with a man. I don't just mean the sex—although I miss that, too—but the companionship, having someone who cares about me. I am surrounded by friends and family having babies—their first, second, or beyond—living as families. That's all I ever really wanted. I'm happy for them, but it hurts to see because I wanted that for me, and especially for Sage. I hope I find it for real someday.

Jim is unbearable to even deal with. He gives me attitude, yells, and hangs up on me constantly. Where does he get off? I'm doing everything—raising Sage, taking care of her every need, working— and he's doing nothing, not giving us a dime. Why is he making this so hard? Seriously, it's like he doesn't give a shit at all. He seems annoyed just to talk to me. He did everything wrong, and I'm chasing him to take some responsibility. He never says he's sorry or tells me he knows what I'm going through or even hints that he cares about us at all. All I get is anger, and then he hangs up or walks out. I feel like I'm the only one grieving for our relationship and he's already moved on, with no regrets about losing me. I keep thinking that can't be true, but his actions say otherwise. I just want him out of my life!

Sorry—enough about that. I know what you mean: this is just the way it is for now, and it will change. It will change. Maybe this is a life lesson for both of us. We're forced to look at ourselves and become self-reliant, and only then will we find someone we really deserve. I don't know.

There was a work meeting with the founder of my school today, and although sometimes I think he may be full of it, I have to say he's inspiring. He talked about setting a goal for one year, visualizing where I want to be in work and in life. He said he tries to look at what was done and what was not done in the past year and then focus on the big picture for the next year. Don't get distracted by the small stuff—it will get done eventually, and in the long run, it's not that important. Focus on what you really want. That is what I want to do.

Luv,
Amanda

Tuesday, January 19, 2010

It's my second week at work, and I'm doing really well. I didn't think I'd be able to enjoy it so much so soon. I like the people I work with. We have a great chef, and the food is all healthy and organic. We get a massage every other week, and they pay for part of my commute. It's a lot of responsibility and I'm very busy, but it's a good place with good people and I like it. I feel needed and genuinely appreciated for the work I do and what I bring to the table. I've been able to help in many ways, and I get so much done in a week that people notice, which is satisfying. The job also has potential. In time I'll probably move up, and the salary will get better. I'm working with like-minded people in health and nutrition, and the school offers a lot to support our well-being at work. For now, and maybe even for the future, it's a great opportunity.

I'm starting to feel more independent and better in general. I'm focused on the now and the future, not the past and what I've been through (though that's helped me to appreciate what I do have). I can spend weekends with Sage and still have a social life. My friends have been incredible, and between them and dating, I'm busy outside of work as well. I feel complete, and I realize with just this little bit of happiness, how very unhappy I was. Something was wrong with me to stay with someone who treated me so poorly. I knew it wasn't right, but I wanted so desperately to make it work that I compromised my own health, happiness, and sanity.

Now the people I choose to be around are good—they lift me up and don't bring me down. I have my bad days, but now I come home, and instead of being depressed, I feel fulfilled and, most of all, safe. I appreciate Sage even more because of all the hard work I have to put in to balance my schedule and be a good mom. I'm doing it on my own with the help of my parents, and it's working: she's okay. We may not have everything, but she's loved and she knows it. I'm not depressed, sad, or angry, and things finally aren't spinning out of control in front of her. We're much happier on our own, without Jim. She has great kids that she gets to spend time with, and she rarely mentions her father, so I know I made the right decision.

I'm starting to feel like myself again, starting to have feelings other than pure sadness. When I speak with Jim, sometimes he upsets me, but it's not the same. I see him differently now. He really lost and was meant to be alone. There's no way anyone can change him. If Sage and I couldn't do it, no one can. I would love to understand him, but I'm starting to care less and less.

Juan helped me out by buying his TV and a few other things for more than I was asking, which was an act of startling kindness. He just wanted to help. I was able to help him, too, by getting work at my office for an electrician friend of his. It feels good to be around good people and be able to give back. It's a breath of fresh air.

When I talk to Jim or his mother, it takes me back to a place I don't want to be. It's toxic—that's the only way I can describe it. She stopped calling me, and when I call her, she is cold and short and lies for Jim. She'll tell me he's out running an errand for her when he's really out for the night. She talks as though the past six months didn't happen at all.

I had thought it might be okay for him to come over to help with Sage before I came home from work, but when I asked my dad, he said no. When I spoke with Jim's mom, she was disappointed; she said I should be sure first before I promise something so Jim won't get upset. She said he had been looking forward to seeing Sage. She actually had the audacity to tell me I should keep my word when it comes to Jim seeing Sage, or Jim might get offended. Is she kidding? He's had years to see her. I need to separate myself from both of them, because they're in a sick relationship right now and she can't pull herself out. She knows he's not giving me a dime, and yet she says nothing about it, to me or to him. I'm over it, over them. Over.

Thursday, January 28, 2010

I shouldn't laugh, but nothing surprises me anymore, and if I don't have a sense of humor about it at this point, then Jim has beaten me. I spoke to one of the men who's been helping him with the supposed Hope Street closing. I'd been pressing Jim for some child- (and wife-) support money—anything—and he finally said he was getting a bridge loan and I could pick up $500 from his mother. I did, and she assured me that the loan was real—but I knew that the money was hers and she was just trying to make him look responsible, probably believing what she wanted to believe.

When I spoke to the guy from the closing, I asked whether Jim really was getting the loan and whether the closing was really going to happen.

He laughed. He said he had spent the day with the lenders, and they discovered they didn't even need Jim to buy the building. He had evidently forged phony agreement papers between him and the bank that was foreclosing on the building, giving him first right of refusal. They don't know how, but he made an intricate bogus document that he's been passing off all this time as his golden ticket, but to restructure the loan now and take Jim out, they would need more time they don't have. He has committed fraud many times over. Ironically, he could actually make out pretty well if everyone around him forces the closing to happen. When I asked about the bridge loan, he said that, yes, Jim had tried hard to get one, claiming he needed money for his family to eat. But the lender was advised by one of the people I have been speaking to, "Don't lend him a dime. I know his wife, and she's a sweetheart—he hasn't given her anything in six months."

He didn't get the loan, so I'll let his mom have fun trying to get her money back. After I picked up the $500—which won't take us far at all—Jim texted to say he wanted to talk to me about seeing Sage; he said he was starting a new night job upstate. He said he'd call the next day. That was two days ago, and I haven't heard a thing.

From: Amanda
Date: Thursday, January 28, 2010 6:27 PM
To: Susan
Subject: Men!

Hey, Sweetie,

Sounds like you had an eventful week.

I met a guy last Saturday when I went over to my friend's house for a drink. He was cute; not that tall, but at least 5'10" and really sweet. Twenty-eight years old. He asked for my number and asked me out. He texted yesterday to say he had a good time and that he's going on vacation and would like to contact me when he gets back. He sounds promising—or at least normal—but I'm wary of even starting anything. He's young, has no kids, living a single life. I don't know how I would integrate into my life someone who doesn't have a child (and therefore couldn't possibly understand my having to focus on Sage as much as I do). I just don't know.

It sounds like you guys will have fun dancing tomorrow. Thanks for the invite, but I'm actually looking forward to pizza night with Sage's girlfriends; I never get to see the moms anymore because I don't pick her up from school.

Good luck talking with your boss tomorrow about work. Remember this, if nothing else: you are awesome and she is lucky to have you! It doesn't matter if you don't know everything. Just pretend you do and wing it, then research it when you get home. Fake it until you make it. Act like you know what you're doing—sound confident! People don't care so much what you say as how you say it; I learned that the hard way.

I really wasn't sure I knew what I was doing at this job at first, but after two weeks, they moved me up into the position of the person they hired me to work for—and she's been here for five months! They said they like that I'm calm, cool, always say I can handle things, and then get things done. I had no idea what I would be doing when I walked in here, but every time I got a challenge, I just took it on and got it done. It's scary at first, but once you do something once, it's not so scary anymore. I have to learn this computer ordering system, and the girl who's teaching me (the one whose position I'm taking) has no idea what she's doing. So I broke it down into small steps, and after a few hours, I felt more comfortable than she ever did. Seriously, the key is to take a big project and break it into manageable steps that you can cross off as you go until you accomplish your goal.

Simplify and take that simple model to your boss. Sound confident, but not complicated.

Luv,
A

Chapter 9: Getting Back Up Again—February 2010

Tuesday, February 2, 2010

I walk around with a void, a space in my chest for Sage. There's no way to fill it. I talk to people, I work, I laugh, and I hope that people don't notice it, don't judge me for it. But it's there.

When I think of Jim now I know what we had is unfinished. What transpired between us is too much for words. I know we will meet again and finish what was started. It may not be now, it may not even be in this lifetime, but it will be. I feel like he is a dead man walking. Jim has destroyed so many lives. He has no idea that the only person that really matters is Sage. Jim stopped calling Sage at the times he promised he would. He is dead inside, dead to me, dead to his child.

I don't want Sage to grow up feeling inferior, the way I did. I don't want to hug her and feel like I did not give her everything she deserves. I laugh with her, spend time with her, and love her unconditionally. I try not to break my promises to her and I hope that it is enough. I have to hope it will be enough.

What we have is unfinished. I will meet you on the other side.

Monday, February 8, 2010

Sometimes I feel like I never learn my lesson. Last week I blew a tire and asked Jim if he remembered the make and model because he had blown two tires a year ago. He said he'd get it fixed for free and have money for me today.

I was at work, and I told him I'd call on my way home and meet him at his friend's tire place. I called, and he texted that he was in a meeting and would call when he was done. I left work early to meet him, and he just kept texting that he'd be done and would call soon. I ran errands and waited in my car, and he avoided my calls until I finally texted that he should just tell me if he couldn't do it because I didn't have time to wait. He wrote back that he couldn't make it—he said he could do it tomorrow, or I could go get my own tire.

I don't know why, but I started to cry. It hurt. I shouldn't have been surprised. I ended up having to go to a tire shop and get my own tire. I texted him that that was fine, but to still bring me the money today. He called me, shouting into the phone that he was the only one supporting our family and that the meeting was *about* money. He said I always ask him for money and he was trying to get some, and now I was complaining about that, too. I said that wasn't the point at all, and that no meeting for money he can't even borrow takes four hours. He said he'd give me money when and if he had it. It's like he was hearing someone else and answering the questions he wanted to answer.

I saw him driving from Brooklyn at eight o'clock this morning while I was waiting for the bus. Yesterday was the Super Bowl, so I can only imagine where he'd been. When I spoke to him a little while ago, he was nasty and rude, not listening to me at all. He sounded like he was on coke. It was familiar. I hope his mother's getting a taste of what I put up with for the last twelve years.

She seems to think he's an angel now, and she's completely abandoned her granddaughter. She doesn't call or ask to see Sage at all anymore. She and Jim are like two peas in a pod: when Sage is out of their sight, she's out of their minds. I hope they're happy together.

Wednesday, February 10, 2010

Sage said to me tonight that she wants to sleep at my parents' house, and that she wants me to sleep there, too. I almost died inside. She said she doesn't know why, but she's just more comfortable there. I asked if it was because there are so many people there, like Grandma, Poppy, Uncle Dax, and Nonna. She said yes. I think what she means is that when she's here, it's just the two of us and she gets lonely. She said I'm always busy—particularly on the phone and computer—and she's right. When I get home, I'm generally occupied: tying up loose ends from the day, cooking, cleaning, doing dishes, talking on the phone, and so on. All of it's necessary, but much of it leaves her feeling ignored and alone.

I told her I wouldn't use the phone or the computer until she was asleep and that we'd eat dinner together every night. It made me sad. She misses having a dad and wants a house full of siblings. I always wanted her to have a big family. I tried, and I'm still trying, but it's a double-edged sword. If I want to meet someone, I have to be out a lot. and then she doesn't see me; yet if I'm with just her all the time, I'll never meet anyone. It's hard to be a single parent and stay balanced. I never want her to feel ignored like I did as a kid. Poor little girl. When she said that, my heart felt like someone was squeezing it. and I had to hold back from crying.

I wish I could do more, but I'm only one person.

Saturday, February 13, 2010

Last night I planned to go out after work, and one of the people that Jim took for a lot of money called as I was about to meet my friends. (I had loaned him the Audi Jim stopped paying for six months ago, because I can't afford the payments—he got it inspected and had the oil changed.) We started talking about Jim, as usual. We talked about cheating, and he mentioned something that I didn't want to hear but asked about anyway. He said about a month ago, Jim asked him if he could borrow some money because he wanted to take a girl to the movies. Jim showed him a picture—she was horribly skinny and looked like a crackhead.

This was just like Jim's father. He owed Jim money and disappeared for a while, then called him out of the blue asking for more money so he could get a hotel room for a girlfriend that was coming to town. Jim saw the insanity of that situation, but he doesn't see the hypocrisy here.

The news hit me like a sucker punch. I went out and got drunk—not sloppy, but enough to dull the pain. I came home and slept for about three hours. When I got up, there was a message from Jim's mom, asking to see Sage. This was too much. In her message she said, "Hello, it's Mom" (she never calls herself "Mom" to me). When I called her back, she sounded falsely upbeat, but I agreed to let her come over and watch Sage while I got my hair cut.

She looked worn. Even into her mid-sixties she had looked very good for her age, with barely a wrinkle, but today she looked like the last two months had aged her twenty years.

"He's not staying with me anymore," she said.

I had a feeling. "What happened?"

She said that a couple weeks ago, Jim had said he had to work nights, but she knew he wasn't working. One night he stayed out all night, and last weekend he didn't come home at all. On Monday, she asked him what was going on. "I said he could live with me or someplace else, but not in-between, not both."

"I tried to warn you. Do you know about his girlfriend?"

She looked shocked and confused. "*Girlfriend?*"

"A friend told me. And the last time I spoke to him, there was a baby crying in the background." I couldn't go on. I started to cry myself.

She touched my shoulder. "Amanda, honey, don't let yourself get upset about this. You have to get over him. He's not adding to this woman's life—or her child's, if she has one. He's not helping her. He's sick.

She continued, "So the next day, he didn't come home again, and I had just had it. Two o'clock in the morning, I called his phone. I expected it to be turned off, but he picked up, wide-awake. I told him, 'I've done everything I can. I don't want you to come back here. I can't help you anymore.' I hung up. I changed the code to the garage. I haven't heard from him since."

"I tried to tell you."

"I know you did. But I had to see for myself. It seemed like he was on the road to recovery. He was taking care of himself—shopping with me, cooking, taking vitamins. But it didn't last. He was killing me, and I told him so. I told him if he went out and did that again, it would be the last time. He would be out of my life forever. And here we are."

"The last time I saw him when I let him see Sage a month ago," I said, "he took a drug test. I'm positive he used someone else's urine. I didn't tell you because you would've thought I was lying. I wanted to protect you, but you wouldn't believe me."

"How could I believe that about my own son? I hadn't lived with him since he left at sixteen. I had to see for myself, as a mother. I'm sorry."

"I understand. He's your son."

"Amanda, I'm dying inside. I'm out of part of my pension because of the money I gave your father for Jim, and I know now Jim won't be able to pay me back. I think he knew that closing wasn't going to happen and he started to fall apart again."

"Don't let him back in with you."

She told me that the next day she let Jim get some of his things when she was not home. He took everything. I had lamps, paintings, china, chairs, valuables, and items that meant so much to me, in my mother-in-law's basement. Jim had but a few boxes, clothes, a computer, desk and personal items. Instead of just taking his things, he took mine, too. My mementos, my whole life was in those boxes. My past was stolen.

I couldn't bear to hear anymore. I couldn't think about where Jim is and what he's doing. Every part of his life is falling apart. He owes everyone, he's maxed out his credit cards, and his bank accounts are all closed. He has nothing, not even gas money for the car. He has millions of dollars in judgments against him. He has no health insurance, and his car insurance is going to run out soon. His friend Joel, who owns the car he's driving, is soon going to have to report the car stolen because Jim hasn't been making payments. He gives nothing to support his daughter, but he has money for cigarettes, booze, drugs, and a girlfriend.

How does he not suffocate?

When I left his mom, I just lost it. I haven't taken a step this far back since he disappeared over three months ago. He's not even pretending to care anymore. He used me to perfect his con, and now he's out there with a girl more suited for him, a fellow addict. He can finally be himself. Like my dad said, he likes that life, really likes it, and now he doesn't have to hide and pretend he wants a wife and family. He told me when we met that all his friends said he would *never* marry, and then he told me that people were stunned when we got engaged. They thought I must have been really something to inspire him to settle down. I was flattered. Now I know he used me. He told me a few months ago that being with me kept him much straighter than he would have been without me. He admitted to holding me hostage, and he conceded that it was selfish.

I want closure—I need it. I've wanted it for such a long time. I cried. For me, but mostly for Sage. Rationally, I knew this was coming. I knew who he was and that he wasn't going to stop and that he didn't really have the capacity to be a father. I guess I've always known that. My head is clear now; it's my heart that needs to catch up. I can't emotionally fathom how he could dismiss his own child. A man can abandon a child and there can still be love there, but he flat-out dismissed her. He's had plenty of time to go to family court for visitation rights. He had every opportunity to see Sage in my presence and to talk with her on the phone. He never did any of those things, and now that he's missing again, it's simple for him: out of sight, out of mind. I texted him a few days back about her report card and her first ice-skating party and got nothing in reply. The only good thing, the only thing that's a relief, is that his mom knows now. At least she has no illusions anymore.

Feeling this way is a setback, but I can't let it overwhelm me. It feels like years of hell coming to an end. I know for certain that he's gone from my life and Sage's. He stole my memories packed up in boxes, and most likely sold them. Those were boxes probably better left unopened anyway. He really is free now from all responsibility—but it will catch up with him one day. At least I don't have to worry about seeing him for Sage's sake. I've grown a lot these past few months—I've made big improvements and had many moments of laughter and peace—but sometimes I can't help but reopen wounds that feel fresh again.

I wanted closure. I needed closure. This was my closure, sent to Jim in a text message:

> This is the last time I will contact you. You wanted your freedom, freedom from your family? You are now free. I hope your new girlfriend and your crack addiction are worth losing your wife and daughter. No girl you are with will ever compare to us. Do not contact us again. Sage is better off without a father like you: a bum, an addict, a liar, and a deserter. I think deep down you know I'm right and that's why you stay away. Don't come near us again. I will tell her you've gone away and are too sick to come back. You are dead to us.

Then it dawned on me. For the past six months, he had not once initiated contact with me—to see Sage or for any other reason—and as far as I can remember in the last year, he never has. I initiated every contact. It shouldn't be that difficult to cut him out of our lives. All I have to do is not call him. It's that simple.

There's no building closing; there is nothing. I am alone in parenting our child, but I am not alone: I have Sage. She is my closure.

Thursday, February 18, 2010

I've had a great week. Work is fantastic. The owner of the company wants to talk to me about becoming a manager, and the projects I'm on are going well;

everyone is impressed. Life is getting better in every respect. I love my job—
it feels like a second home. I love the people and the whole atmosphere. It's
amazing how life can change.

Ever since I texted Jim that he should never contact me again, he's been
texting me every day, but I don't respond. He threatens that he's going to
take me to court. Let him! I can't wait to see his argument. I will meet him
there with bells on.

The other night I met with someone I've known through Jim for a long time,
and it really helped me to move on. His friend Mike loaned him over $1 mil-
lion, which is now gone. Mike is different from Jim. He's genuine, sweet, and
caring. I told him everything, and he really listened to me. He grew up with
Jim and had trusted him implicitly, but that trust had been fading; I told him
a lot that confirmed what he already suspected. I always liked Mike—he's
funny and smart, and we always got along well.

He's another person Jim kept me away from out of fear he might talk to
me about what was really going on. He told Mike recently that I had brain
cancer. (*Him, too?*) He said I didn't want anyone to know, and begged him
not to talk about it with anyone, even his mother—who happens to be best
friends with Jim's mother. I asked Mike how on earth he could believe such
a thing, and he said it never occurred to him to doubt it until now. *Brain
Cancer?*

Then he told me Jim admitted to cheating on me years ago with Naudia,
the stripper call girl he had kept in contact with. Mike said all those times
Jim disappeared and went to Atlantic City, he was with her. I cried, and he
held me. If there was ever a moment for me to move on, this was it. A clean
break with a clear conscious. A new life.

We spent the night together, and it was amazing. It felt *real.* I don't expect
anything to come of it, but I felt things I hadn't felt in a long time. In one
night, I felt more real than I ever did with Jim.

One of my good friends sent me this quote, and I have to say it has helped me. I printed it out and posted it on the wall of my office. I read it every day, sometimes more than once:

> There comes a point in your life when you realize who matters, who never did, who won't anymore, and who always will, so don't worry about the people from your past—there's a reason why they didn't make it into your future. Tomorrow is a privilege, so live today like tomorrow isn't happening.

Sunday, February 21, 2010

Sage spent the week at my parents' house, and although I truly missed her, it was a great relief. For just a week, I felt young again. I felt like I had freedom and little responsibility. It was a much-needed break, and I felt like a single woman again. Slowly but surely, I'm on my road to recovery.

> *I can finally heal, move on, breathe, and have a chance at finding someone else. I feel a sense of sanity I haven't felt in years.*

I haven't seen Mike since last week, and we haven't spoken. I do like him, but I can't chase anyone and I won't be available to someone just physically. I don't regret anything, but if we do talk again, it won't be me initiating it. I'm not used to men keeping me at a distance. I know I'm probably not ready for a relationship, that is not what I want from him, but this felt real.

I can see why it's probably difficult for Mike to be around me. I'm a single mom, and the reason he's struggling right now is the money he gave to Jim, and I'm a part of that. I am the wife of the man who financially ruined his life. Of course, I didn't know it at the time, but I can't help but know now that the reason we had such a comfortable life was because of people like Mike. Everything we had was directly related to what they gave us.

I don't know how he's able to feel for me, and I guess that's one reason

I have always liked him so much: he has heart. He's not bitter or angry with me, but sympathizes with me, and especially with Sage. I could easily fall in love with someone like him, but I know that it could never really work: I would always feel like he could be secretly bitter. I do like him, though. I like him a lot, but I don't know, nor do I want to ask him, how he feels. I just know right now I want him in my life because I haven't had feelings like this for anybody in so long. But I'm not willing to put my heart at risk. I can't afford to get hurt. Not now.

Love *is* hurt. Relationships are messy, and I have to give my heart to get back love, but first I need to rebuild. I need to make sure I'm healed before I put myself out there again. Mike's a player, no doubt about it. He probably genuinely feels bad for me, but I think we were both only looking for one thing, and we got it; to hurt Jim. As far as what I want goes, at this point in my life, I'm incapable of bullshit: life doesn't always give us what we want when we want it, and I'm okay with that. I'm not willing to get hurt, not right now.

Wednesday, February 24, 2010

Today I went to work. I was rushing off the bus to my building, and I stopped. I just stopped, right in the middle of the bustle of people with their serious faces running to their jobs. I smiled and I looked up at the sky and I felt grateful. I was grateful that I've made it this far. I went through what felt like hell, and I made it out alive. I'm okay—I really am okay.

> *This is a moment I won't get back. I'm not going to run through life anymore. I'm going to enjoy every moment … when I can.*

I've finally gotten Jim out of my life, out of my head, and for the past two weeks, he's been sending me texts and e-mails threatening to take me to court. A month ago, it would have devastated me; now it barely bothers me at all.

The best thing is that I don't fear much anymore. Being with Jim, I was afraid of being alone, and being without him, I was afraid I couldn't make it. I hid behind people all my life and was afraid to stand up on my own two feet. The brief times I did, it felt wonderful, but then I would go right back into my shell. I hid behind Jim for twelve years, and no one knew me for who I really was. But I don't have to be afraid anymore, because my worst fears have already come true and I'm still here, better and brighter, more appreciative and humbler than ever.

Now I'm complimented left and right, not based on what people know I've been through, but simply on who I am today. I'm wiser. I am strong, confident, loyal, and compassionate, and it's obvious to those around me. The head of my company wants me to work as his personal assistant. In the past, I might have been afraid to tell him what I wanted and didn't want. But I'm not afraid anymore. If I feel unsure, I just look back—not to cry about what's happened, but to know that if I can survive that, I can survive anything. The past is a reminder of what I don't want to become and of what I know I will never be again. It had its purpose, and it serves that purpose in my life today.

I am not afraid. I am living and living and living.

Thursday, February 25, 2010

I listened to a meditation last night, and it told me to keep asking the questions I want the answers to. Will Sage be okay without a father? Will I find someone in my life that will be as good to her as he is to me, someone who will appreciate her like I do? Will I find someone who will take extra care of me? Someone who will hold me and make Sage and me feel safe? Will I have a man in my life who wants a family? Will I be able to build a life with him? Will I have more children? Will our love grow over the years instead of dissipate? Will I ever feel safe again?

Is that enough questions? Because I have more.

I'm lonely again tonight. I can feel it like a knot in my side. I've been lonely for years, but with distractions. Those distractions are growing distant, and now I'm left with myself, whom I have to look at more often than I would like. People keep saying this is all part of it and I'm just getting stronger. Well, I hope there's virtue in my suffering.

I'm out to learn more about who I really am. I'm out to find someone who will know me, the me I really was before, the me I want to be again.

Sunday, February 28, 2010

Richard called on Friday: *there will be no Hope Street closing.* Someone else bought the building, and there's no more waiting. It's over. *It is finally over!* And do you know what?

I don't care.

Jim will just have to deal with his past and the people he owes. At least I can file for an uncontested divorce now. I was waiting for the closing, to see if there was any money to actually fight for.

I texted him this morning:
I have a lawyer who can get us an uncontested divorce for $650. We both have nothing, and I don't want anything from you—just child support. I need this to be over. Just split the cost with me and sign. Let's get it done this week.

He texted back:
Not without visitation for Sage.

I texted:

> That we have to go to court for. It has nothing to do with the divorce. *Uncontested* means we both just split with nothing. I'm the only one losing here. If you make money on anything you started while we were married, I won't get a dime. I just want out. After you go to rehab, we can make arrangements for you to see Sage, supervised. I just want the divorce.

He texted:

> I want nothing more than to help. Things have been really tight for me. I am far from living well. I've been working and starting a new business. I'll do whatever you want. It's going to take a little time for me to get a cushion, and then I'll help all I can. Please tell Sage I miss her and love her. I know you don't believe in me anymore, but I'm not giving up. I'll be back on my feet soon. I cry for her all the time and will do all I can to help you and her.

I texted:

> You have a choice whether to help with our daughter; I don't—she has to eat. You are my past, and there are reasons why you didn't make it into my future. By the way, I know about you and Naudia. If you don't want to give me your new address, I'll send the papers to her house, I know who to get her address from.

He texted:

> You can believe whatever you want to believe, but I don't and haven't talked to Naudia. I'll forward my address when I move in. And pick up the phone if what you have to say is so important—stop texting me! If I am your past, then act like it.

I texted:

> I don't want to hear your voice anymore. You are my past, and the divorce will make you a distant memory.

His life is over. No one I know will work with him or lend him money, and I'm sure I won't see a dime. The divorce is just the last nail in the coffin of our life together; we've been over for a long time—longer, I think, than I realized.

The love and hurt I felt for Jim is gone, dead. I feel nothing for him. I'm happier than I've been in a long time, and I want these feelings to crystallize so he can't ever creep up on me again. Any hope for a good life with him, just like the Hope Street pot of gold, is over.

I'm not sad about getting divorced. I'm just aggravated that I have to deal with him to get one. With or without a man in my life, I am now free. I don't have to worry about being lied to or manipulated, or feeling like I'm living in an alternate reality anymore. I know what I have now. I work hard for what I get, and I know where it's coming from and where it's going.

It's not about control anymore. I always wanted to control things to make me feel safe, but it's about letting go now. People will do as they please, and trying to control the future only makes for a present that is unbearable. Living in the present, appreciating the now, and having goals for the future are the only plans I can make. I'm alone with my daughter and I'm practically penniless and *I am fine*. The good things in my life are abundant and obvious now, and in time, I'm sure I'll even learn to appreciate the past. I experienced things I might never have experienced, I lived a life that not many get to live, and I learned a lot. I'm a better person for it now.

This is just the beginning, and already there's a weight lifted from my shoulders, a heavy burden I put on myself that I can now let go of. It's okay to let go; it's okay to leave when something isn't right. I need to take care of myself, and it's all right to be alone. I tried recently to fill the void in my life with men, and it didn't work.

Only I can fill that void.

Chapter 10: Sometimes the Weak Become the Strong—May 2010

Saturday, May 1, 2010

I recently started dating someone I think I like. Ron is ten years older than me, divorced, has two kids, and is a really great person. He's successful, smart, funny, attentive, and attractive. At first he called and texted me constantly, which ordinarily would have been a big turnoff. But he's growing on me. I *like* that he calls me all the time, I *like* that he's a great dad, and I *like* that he's such a good person. Of course, we barely know each other, and my world has been upside-down for months, if not years, but so far this feels good.

Jason wanted to meet him and check him out. I guess with the mistakes I made in my last relationship, I need approval for future ones. He said he can read any guy. He swung by my place before we were heading out for a date, and after fifteen minutes, he gave me the thumbs-up.

I'm not ashamed of what happened to me, but I'm still getting used to not having what I used to; sometimes it's difficult to know that I can't just buy anything I want anymore. I'm also wary of giving myself to anyone, and I've been very guarded with every guy I've dated so far. I've always let the guy chase me because that's my nature, but recently I've been even more distant, and I'm trying to open up. I don't know when I'll be able to fully trust again, but I think I'm getting there.

I've been on a few dates recently and felt no spark, but there's something about this guy that makes me want to be with him. That in itself is a scary feeling. It feels good, but I'm not ready to be hurt again. I need honesty, and it seems like the beginning of a relationship involves a lot of games. I've played so many games and danced around with Jim for so long …

I just want to be with someone who will be straight with me.

I had another date last night with the brother of a friend. She's been trying to set us up for a while. He's forty-three, really good-looking, tall, in great shape, funny, and really nice … but again, there weren't many sparks on my end. I reluctantly saw him a second time, though, and I'm glad I did. He's refreshing—a little immature because of his single lifestyle, but open about liking me and wanting to see me. He's serious about getting married and having kids, and he has no baggage from past relationships.

For the first time in my life, I'm torn: I can't decide whom I like better, or who would be better for me. I guess I'll just see them both for now and see what happens. I deserve this. I deserve two men wanting me after what I've been through.

I don't know where Jim is, but the last we spoke, he said he'd sign the divorce papers, which is all I want. He's getting no money from the building—nothing. He's done, just a junkie scamming people for cash. I want nothing to do with him. He said he'd come in and sign the papers, and then he didn't answer his calls all day and then texted me an address that doesn't even exist to put on the paperwork! Why even give it to me? I just wanted to cry in frustration.

Can't he just let me go?

Monday, May 3, 2010

I had a good and busy weekend. I slept over at Ron's house. We had a good time, and I feel really comfortable with him. There are some red flags, though:

he really keeps me separate from his family life, in a way that makes me wonder if he'll ever let anyone inside. He also complains a lot about his ex-wife. I don't know. We're not serious, but I don't want to waste my time and I don't want to make another mistake. I can't afford to make any more mistakes. I know he really likes me—he says he misses me when we're apart—but it seems like there's just not enough room for me in his life.

Dating is exhausting. I can't wait to find and develop a real relationship. That's why Mike is so much more appealing: he's ready; he told me; he wants to be married and have kids. Then again, he hasn't walked the walk. He may very well want those things now, but what happens once he really gets them? When things get tough, I don't know if he's the type to be a real man and stay. I can't tell yet.

Tuesday, May 11, 2010

Mike spent the night at my apartment last night. I didn't expect anything to happen, but we connected and I didn't resist. He wasn't what I was expecting—he was actually very sweet and gentle. It was refreshing.

I'm leaving work in a few minutes to go sign the divorce papers at the attorney's office. I'm sweating, nervous to see Jim. It's been four months since I have laid eyes on him.

I think of all the sad songs he made me listen to throughout our relationship, after a fight, and before he started disappearing, when I still had some hope for him, songs that reflected how sorry he was for hurting me, how he's such a tortured soul. He said the songs spoke for him better than he could himself; by asking me to listen to them, he was asking me to believe in him. The prevailing message was that sometimes the weak become the strong. He wanted me to believe that he was really going to be strong, and I wanted to believe in him. But you know something? It turns out it was me who became strong. It's my life, my choice, my words, and my voice. Now I realize it was me.

I was supposed to believe in me.

Tuesday, May 11, 2010, evening

He came. Jim came to the attorney's office. He signed the paperwork. He walked up to the building in fresh, clean, jeans and a button-down shirt, but he looked awful. He had a cigarette in his mouth, and he looked older. He had gained weight and was clean-shaven, with no goatee, which accentuated his weak chin and chubby face. He walked in, shook the attorney's hand, and sat down. He was serious and curt. It felt like a business transaction. We barely spoke, but he signed on every line and initialed every page. He didn't contest much, and he only spoke when spoken to.

I was five dollars short to pay the attorney, and I had to beg Jim to help me out. True to form to the very end, he claimed he had nothing. Then he pulled out a wad of cash and finally put a five on the table. What a bargain it was for him, five bucks for a divorce. To me, the price was about right for our marriage—and it was poetic that in the end, I finally got him to pay for something.

Cutting the cords from the destruction and ruin he brought into my life was the best thing I've ever experienced. He's weak and pathetic now—not strong, not whole, not real, not human. He said, once again, that he was going to take me to court over Sage, but I have a feeling that this is the last I'll be seeing of him. I could hardly refrain from smiling. What I thought might be sad and distressing was actually one of the most freeing moments I've ever experienced.

I called Richard and told him the good news—he was ecstatic for me. He was doubtful that Jim did this out of the goodness of his heart, and he was probably right. His "girlfriend" probably made him do it. Well, good for her. I told Richard I didn't care how it was done—as long as I was free of him, I was happy. Someday I would thank that woman personally.

Ron had been skeptical that Jim would even show up. I texted him after it was over: It's done. And I'm smiling now. He called and I told him everything, and he was happy for me. I was happy for me. I felt like I had just escaped from the brink of death, and I let out a shout in my car that made me shiver with joy. I wanted to kiss the ground, upon which I was now able to walk free.

Sometimes the weak do become the strong.

Wednesday, May 12, 2010

I wrote this e-mail to Jim today, not for him but for me:

From: Amanda
Date: Wednesday, May 12, 2010 7:36 AM
To: Jim
Subject: Thank you

Jim,

What you did yesterday was the most noble thing you have ever done for me. I really mean that. You set me free yesterday, allowing me to move on with my life. And you helped Sage, too: a happy mom makes a happy child.

Whatever you think of me, I'll leave you with this: my intentions were always the best. You're still the father of my child. I never wanted to see you fall this low; it saddens me. But I realize now that you were right: you kept me because with me you were at least trying to be a better person. I brought you up, you brought me down, and we met somewhere in the middle, which is why it worked for so long.

You may not care about any of this, but I have to thank you. You taught me a lesson. You made me appreciate the simpler things in life; you made me appreciate what I do have, who is in my life, who really loves and cares about me. I no longer wake up with a knot in my stomach. I'm free to have a normal, happy life, and now for the first time, I know I deserve it.

I know you have a problem—nobody normal could treat people the way you have and feel no remorse. I know you can't help it; it's who you are and you don't even see it. You don't have the capacity to feel sorry for what you've done because you don't actually think what you did was wrong.

So, thank you for yesterday. Thank you for the lessons you've taught me. I wish you the best in your life.

Amanda

Fifteen minutes after I sent this, Richard called to tell me he just saw Jim and his new girlfriend. Early twenties, tall, thin, and cute, with big, fake boobs. He said she looked like a stripper. The only thing that hurts is knowing that since he's with her, he'll probably never give me anything for Sage. But if she's the one who got him to sign the papers, I'm still grateful, and it's also a bonus that if he's focused on her, he won't bother me.

Actually I feel sorry for her. Nothing he did to me is her fault. He's been parading her around like a trophy to his friends, and he's probably giving her the same line that he gives everyone else: he's struggling, his wife left him with nothing, and as soon as he closes Hope Street, he'll take care of her beyond her wildest dreams. If she can just help him a little bit now, it would be great because he really loves her. He's a leech and a con, and she has no idea what she's in for. He's under her control for now, but that girl just got into bed with the devil. She'll find out soon enough.

I'm okay and Sage is okay, and that's all that matters to me.

Tuesday, May 18, 2010

I really feel like I'm a different person now—I can't imagine myself with Jim anymore, yet it wasn't long ago that I couldn't picture a life without him. When I tried to, I thought I'd never find anybody. Even as I wrote in these pages that one day I would get over this, there were many times I didn't really believe it myself. I felt like I would never get away from the sadness and depression. I just couldn't picture being happy as a single, working mom. It seemed like something in a dream, so distant and so foreign from my life.

The only bad feeling that remains now is knowing Jim is out there with a young girlfriend and not his daughter. I had hoped that he would at least not fall into a new relationship and would use what money he did have for Sage, but let's face it: he's addicted, so how offended can I be?

I, on the other hand, have two amazing guys I am dating. My biggest challenge now is balance, a far cry from where I was a year ago. I'm trying to work full-time, attend to Sage, run errands, and see friends and date, all while trying to keep track of and fulfill my goals in life—it's difficult. But I'll take these hardships over my old life any day.

I just feel so overwhelmed with happiness and appreciation sometimes that I want to scream. I can't believe it took me so long to realize life could be this way. I didn't realize life had so much potential.

Last weekend was my birthday, and my company took us to a yoga retreat in the Berkshires. It was a much-needed weekend of "me time"—relaxation, exercise, fresh air, and bonding with great people from work. I laughed so hard I cried; I went hiking and took yoga and breathing classes; I sat in the sauna, ate healthy food, and just got away from everything.

I felt guilty about leaving Sage and missing her Spring Concert, but I needed this and I enjoyed every second. It's just another step in the growing process I'm in. I have a lot and I've learned a lot, and now I'm just connecting the dots. I'm realizing that I need to take more time for me instead of running around all the time trying to do everything. I eat well and I'm thin, but I need to exercise more. Exercise of any kind, whether it's hiking, yoga, or even just walking, is regenerative, and if I need anything right now, it's regeneration.

I know what I want and what I don't want, and I'm not afraid to be myself or to let the men in my life know how I feel. I deserved this past weekend, and I deserve to date men who are good to me. I deserve time for myself. I spent the first five years of Sage's life being with her around the clock. My job's far from over, but I don't have to feel guilty if I take a little time for myself. After all, what's that they tell you on airplanes? Put on your own oxygen mask first? If I can't breathe, I can't help her. Plus, she's safe with my parents, and I'm there with her as much as I can be. The time we spend together is wonderful; I don't have to feel like I'm a bad mother just because I can't be with her as much as I used to. (Okay, busted: clearly I'm feeling some guilt, or I wouldn't be writing this.) Someday soon I'll be with her a lot more again.

I walked alone for a long time, as if my feet were not my own. That's a path I chose. There are doors I've opened and closed. I'm choosing to close one behind me right now, and I'm not looking back. I'm looking at another door that's always been open right in front of me, but I couldn't see it until now.

I'm putting one foot in front of the other—my foot.

Sunday, May 30, 2010

I made pancakes this morning! For the first time in six months, I woke up and made pancakes for Sage and me. She helped stir the batter, and we ate them with maple syrup and butter; they were the best I've ever had. This afternoon we're going to walk to the park, and that's all that either of us wants from this day.

After Writing This Book—
Saturday, June 25, 2011

I struggled with writing anything after finishing this journal. I thought about many different ways to approach writing about my life more than a year later. I thought about making it upbeat, positive, possibly sad, but to plan it would be too contrived and that would contrast with the entire journal. There is no one tone. What I feel is bittersweet.

So many things have crossed my mind, gone in and out of my life, changed, transformed, and stayed the same over the last year. I regret that I was too busy to journal anything, but to be quite honest, I was too busy living, making up for lost time, and catching up career-wise and financially. It has been a struggle and a pleasure.

Bittersweet—bitter and sweet.

As far as my contact with Jim, there has been none. I hear stories from time to time of how bad he is doing and how he continues to live the same life. His mother still defends and protects him and asks me why I don't give him supervised visits with Sage, but I have not heard these requests from him at all. In fact, the only contact he made was texting our daughter on Christmas and Easter, saying happy holidays, Daddy loves you, and nothing more. He hasn't tried to see her, go to court, call her, write her a letter, or give her any financial support. It has been almost two years since he has even really been in her life. She asks about him but hardly ever and seems to be thriving despite his absence.

In the last two weeks, I heard from a friend that he went to see Jim after not hearing from him for months. Jim met him a few blocks from where I live in a truck with what few belongings he had left, homeless and destitute, asking this friend for $5,000, then at least $20. This is a person he took hundreds of thousands of dollars from. My friend, having been fooled by Jim so many times before, emptied his pockets before meeting with him so he would have no money to give. Jim told him there was a fire in his apartment, he has nothing, no one will speak to him anymore, not even people he owes money to will pick up the phone. He claims he has nobody, no girlfriend, no one to help him, and he admitted to losing everything, including his wife and child. He said he fucked up but he is not on drugs anymore.

The next day Jim's mom called my father and told him Jim hit rock-bottom. He had nowhere to go and came to her; she let him shower there but not live with her. She said his only option was to go away to rehab, and having no alternative, he reluctantly agreed. His brother drove him to a men's shelter hours away. The next day I got a call from Richard, asking me if I knew Jim was in a rehab and he told me where. His mother had kept that part a secret, but at least I know there is some validity to this claim.

At first I felt sad, genuinely sad. Tears welled up in my eyes, and I was ready all over again to give my feelings and my sympathy to him. I knew it would come to this, and even though I expected it, it was still hard to hear. How did my husband and the father of my child go from living an extraordinary life to homelessness in less than two years? I never, ever, ever would have believed he was like every other addict. He seemed so much smarter, so much more aware of, so educated about addiction and the mistakes that were made before him. I learned the hard way that addiction must run its course and sometimes that course can be a lifetime.

I still know Jim, I do, and I know this is not rock-bottom for him. He didn't want to go away; he just had no choice. He had no other person who would help him, so he went home and his mother did what she always does—picks him up when he is on his last leg right before he is ready to fall. I had been guilty of that for years; only now am I realizing I should have just left. I should not have tried so hard; I should have let his addiction run its course—but so goes the cycle of addiction and the cruelty of coaddiction.

A month or so into his stay, there was a warrant out for Jim's arrest. He surrendered at the suggestion of his rehab counselor. He is currently in prison on $200,000 dollars, which has not been posted. He is awaiting trial sometime in a few months for more than forty counts of felony charges for grand larceny, conspiracy, fraud, and a violent crime he committed a year ago. The main charges are for a mortgage scam he was a part of with a lawyer and a rabbi from 2006. The charges are not even for the crimes he committed with Hope Street—money laundering, conspiracy, fraud, embezzlement, and more in the last four years.

It is a good feeling to know that he is at least finally being held responsible for what he has done.

Even though I know he left me, child in my arms, with dangerous people looking for him, I still felt badly. I wanted to cry, but the tears would not come. In fact, I haven't cried at all in the last year; I can't cry anymore. I have nothing left for him.

I think about him from time to time, and as with all things, the horror starts to fade, and sometimes the good memories resurface. I have pictures, so many pictures, physical and mental samples that there was an "us," but as each day passes, it feels more and more like a dream. It feels like a story I have inside me, but that no one else has read. I question how much I should keep from my daughter and how much I should share with her, and maybe one day I will share the whole story. Maybe one day, I will let her know the whole truth, but these days I just want her to be a normal kid, not scarred from the mistakes her parents have made.

In the time that I have not written, I met a wonderful man. He is the polar opposite of Jim and the type of person I specifically asked for.

I recently looked at the goals I had written for myself, and I realized I have accomplished every single one. Michael asked me to marry him after four months, we bought a beautiful house in the middle of farmland, where Sage has a beautiful home again, space, her own room, a place to play, and all of the things I knew I wanted for her again. I contributed to the house with my own money this time. Shortly after, I learned I was pregnant, and now I am five months pregnant with a little boy and so happy to be having another child. I am so happy to be able to give Sage a brother.

Career-wise, I have been able to prove myself and move up the ladder rather quickly to attain the position that I was always afraid I couldn't. Unlike before, I put up no glass ceilings. I now know that I can do anything. I can accomplish anything. I don't need a man or a job or limitations to define me. I can do exactly what I set out to achieve. I just have to believe it. Every single positive thought and desire I put in my mind and wrote down quickly became part of my instant reality; and from there, I had no choice but to follow the path that would take me there.

I found someone who has all of the attributes I swore I would want in a partner this time. He is everything I asked for, but the best part is he is not perfect. He is thoughtful, honest, loyal, handsome, fit, and energetic; he loves to challenge himself, yet is down to earth and family-oriented, has no hang-ups or baggage that keep us at a distance, and can be very funny and cute when he wants to be. He has no issues with any type of addiction, and most of all, we have a healthy relationship. I am not defined by him, and when we are apart, I don't question his whereabouts or what he is up to. I can breathe with him. I can be myself and not get caught up in what it is he might be hiding.

The thing to understand is that the change has really come from me. I know he is not perfect, nor am I; our relationship is not free from issues and conflict, but that is the best part. I know perfection is not real, and his faults and mine are okay. In fact, my love for him is different this time. He, never being engaged before, having any children, and basically being a bachelor most of his life, told me, "When you know, you just know." He had thought for me it was not the same, that I just wanted stability this time.

He was right in that my feelings for him were different. I would never want to love anyone the way I loved Jim. With Jim it was an insecure love, a sickness that grew as the years passed. The way I love Michael is real, tangible, and steady. I see a future with him; I feel a connection with him. I feel like we are together and that there is no drama or intentional destruction between us. My love for Jim was painful and scary; my love for Michael I can compare to waking up on the most beautiful spring day, sun shining and cool breeze blowing through my window, with the smell of lavender in the air. With him, I feel like I am part of something; and with Jim, I felt alone. It is true that I want stability but in a good way; I still want adventure and fun and excitement, and I know I can have all of those things too.

Michael has made the comment that having a child and a house and everything we are doing is not the same for me because I have done it before. Maybe to some degree this is true, but I can explain that it is very different this time. I actually know that it will go somewhere and that I have a partner, someone who will be there for me and be a good father. He has been a better father to Sage in the last year than Jim was her whole life.

Even though I had the child, the house, and the marriage, it was never real. I was never really able to take part in it the way most people do. Now I feel differently. I feel happy and hopeful, and it is wonderful this time and therefore just as new to me as it is to him. This time I know I am not alone. I know that the person I am with is not so distracted with his addiction that he is always one foot out the door.

For me, I know there will be more to come, and that it is not over with Jim. He is Sage's father, and as long as he exists and his mother is around to take care of him, then there will come a time I may have to deal with him again. I know it is there, but there is nothing I can do but cross that bridge when I come to it. I can't worry or suffer in fear. I won't let fear rule my decisions like they have in the past. I will fight if I have to, but this time I know that it won't break me; after all is said and done, I am responsible only for my own actions and for the safety and care of my children.

I plan to work from home more and to go back to achieve my masters in health and nutrition, my other passion, after the baby is born. I have always wanted to run my own wellness center or be a part of a wellness facility that heals people—mind, body, and spirit. I have written cookbooks and other materials, as well as coached many people into living a healthier life, but I was always missing something. I focused on the food, and what I was missing personally was the most important piece: a healthy emotional state. I rarely touched on this because I didn't have it to give. How can you be healthy when your life is in turmoil constantly? I wasn't, and I know although I am not an expert at it and may never be, I have come a long way and have something to offer.

The world can be cruel and unfair and people and places not what they seem, but I leave that situation wiser, stronger, more independent, capable, and with less fear, self-doubt, worry, and sadness, and finally with more hope. I have come into my new life with a renewed hope.

Hope is a *belief* in a positive outcome in the events and *circumstances* in our lives. Hope is the feeling that what is wanted can be had or that events will turn out for the best. Hope is looking on the brighter side. I can breathe today because I have my hope back and no one can ever take that feeling away from me again. I wake up each day with hope. I let go and hope for the best. Hope, in my opinion, is the sweetest word.

37050785R00123

Made in the USA
Middletown, DE
21 November 2016